SPOTLIGHT

D1569359

SEDONA

KATHLEEN BRYANT

Contents

SEDONA

© KATHLEEN BRYANT

SEDONA AND RED ROCK COUNTRY

Locals like to quip, "God created the Grand Canyon, but He lives in Sedona." Named "the most beautiful place in America" by *USA Today,* Sedona encompasses crimson spires and mesas, evergreen woodlands, and sparkling Oak Creek. The landscape is simply stunning, especially when the stone monoliths and sheer cliffs are burnished by the setting sun.

Sedona's red- and buff-colored rocks mark the southern rim of the Colorado Plateau, a massive expanse of land that rises 2,000 feet from the high-desert floor and stretches into Utah, Colorado, and New Mexico. The colorful stone layers underlying the plateau are revealed here, shaped by geological forces into blocky formations and delicate spires that seem to defy gravity.

The evocative terrain attracts an eclectic following of visitors and residents. Hikers, climbers, and mountain bikers of all skill levels come to scale the colossal buttes, while photographers and painters hope to be inspired by their beauty. Spiritual pilgrims, too, are drawn by the landscape; many believe it is marked by centers of spiraling energy, called vortexes. For others, the scenery merely serves as a magnificent backdrop for golf games, Southwestern cuisine, and rejuvenating spa treatments.

Sedona's fame as a travel destination belies its relatively small size. Situated about 90

© KATHLEEN BRYANT

© KATHLEEN BRYANT

Red Rock Scenic Byway

minutes north of Phoenix, the 19-square-mile community can be divided into three distinct areas: the Village of Oak Creek, Uptown, and West Sedona. Just north is Oak Creek Canyon, a shady retreat with campgrounds, picnic areas, swimming holes, and Slide Rock State Park. To the southwest lies the Verde Valley and Jerome.

Visitors driving from Phoenix on State Route 179 will arrive first in the Village of Oak Creek, an unincorporated area of golf resorts, shopping centers, hotels, and restaurants. The village or VOC, as it's often known, is a handy option for exploring the red rocks and feels pleasantly less congested than the rest of Sedona.

Continue north on State Route 179, known as Red Rock Scenic Byway, and you'll see prominent formations like Bell Rock, Courthouse Butte, and The Nuns. Once you cross over the leafy banks of Oak Creek, you'll arrive at "the Y," a three-pronged intersection that splits West Sedona and Uptown. Touristy Uptown commands impressive views and caters to visitors by offering a diverse selection of accommodations, restaurants, galleries, and shops. You'll find locals, as well as less-expensive hotels and popular bars and bistros, in West Sedona.

Though it can be hard at times to look beyond the hordes of shoppers, convoys of brightly painted tour Jeeps, and storefronts hawking time-shares or psychic readings, none of these can distract from the magical landscape. After all, no matter where you go or what you do in Sedona, the red rocks are a constant presence, reminding you that everything else is a mere blip on the grand geological scale that resulted in this very special place.

PLANNING YOUR TIME

Sedona makes a terrific getaway, whether you have a day or a week, offering scenic beauty and interesting sites within a relatively compact area. The city has developed to accommodate legions of tourists, and its pedestrian-friendly

HIGHLIGHTS

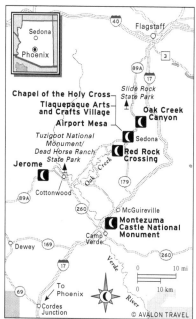

Airport Mesa: Enjoy a bird's-eye view of the red rocks from the top of Airport Mesa, and see if you can recognize Chimney Rock, Capitol Butte, Steamboat, and other colorfully eroded formations (page 11).

Red Rock Crossing: Behold what's said to be the most photographed view in Arizona: the majestic spires of Cathedral Rock rising above Oak Creek at Crescent Moon Ranch Picnic Area. Find the right spot, and you'll see them reflecting in the creek's clear waters (page 12).

Tlaquepaque Arts and Crafts Village: Visit Sedona's charming art-focused shopping village, inspired by Colonial Mexico. It boasts some of the city's best shops, galleries, and restaurants (page 20).

Oak Creek Canyon: Drive the scenic highway through this leafy refuge north of Sedona. The quiet, wooded setting is an ideal place to take a hike. Kids will want to slip down the natural chute at Slide Rock State Park (page 46).

Jerome: Explore this hillside mining town perched above the Verde Valley, which locals like to say is haunted. The narrow streets that were once home to saloons and brothels now feature small restaurants, galleries, and shops (page 51).

Montezuma Castle National Monument: Discover one of the best-preserved cliff dwellings in the country. The five-story, 20-room pueblo, which clings to side of a limestone wall 75 feet above the ground, is an impressive testament to the ingenuity of the prehistoric Sinagua culture (page 63).

LOOK FOR **〔** TO FIND RECOMMENDED SIGHTS, ACTIVITIES, DINING, AND LODGING.

Chapel of the Holy Cross: Admire this iconic church, which appears to rise from the red rocks in a brilliant union of art, nature, and God. Its quiet interior is the perfect place to contemplate Sedona's majestic landscape (page 10).

---

shopping areas, varied restaurants, and intriguing galleries—backdropped by gorgeous red rocks—make getting around easy and fun.

Couples yearning for a romantic weekend can easily pop up from Phoenix for an overnight stay at one of Sedona's charming resorts or inns. More adventurous travelers, though, may want to stay longer in order to explore the natural beauty and historic sites throughout the Verde Valley. Sedona is a convenient home base for scenic drives to fascinating archaeological sites or the mining town of Jerome. Outdoor lovers could easily spend days hiking and biking forest trails, playing golf or tennis, investigating vortex sites, or kayaking down Oak Creek to a wine-tasting room.

No matter what time of year you visit, Sedona's landscape is enchanting. When

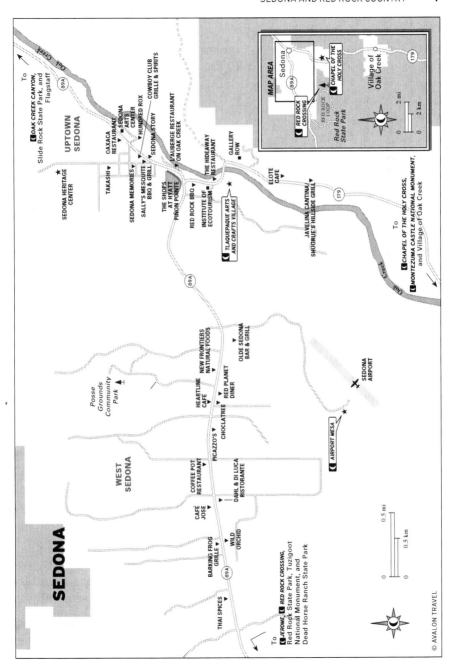

SEDONA

MAP AREA

Sedona

Village of Oak Creek

RED ROCK CROSSING

CHAPEL OF THE HOLY CROSS

Red Rock State Park

2 mi

2 km

To OAK CREEK CANYON, Slide Rock State Park, and Flagstaff

Oak Creek

UPTOWN SEDONA

SEDONA HERITAGE CENTER

TAKASHI

OAXACA RESTAURANT

SEDONA ARTS CENTER

HUNDRED ROX

COWBOY CLUB GRILLE & SPIRITS

L'AUBERGE RESTAURANT ON OAK CREEK

SEDONA STORY

SEDONA MEMORIES

SALLY'S MESQUITE BBQ & GRILL

THE HIDEAWAY RESTAURANT

THE SHOPS AT HYATT PIÑON POINTE

RED ROCK BBQ

INSTITUTE OF ECOTOURISM

GALLERY ROW

ELOTE CAFE

TLAQUEPAQUE ARTS AND CRAFTS VILLAGE

JAVELINA CANTINA/ SHUGRUE'S HILLSIDE GRILL

179

To CHAPEL OF THE HOLY CROSS, MONTEZUMA CASTLE NATIONAL MONUMENT, and Village of Oak Creek

Oak Creek

89A

NEW FRONTIERS NATURAL FOODS

OLDE SEDONA BAR & GRILL

HEARTLINE CAFE

RED PLANET DINER

Posse Grounds Community Park

SEDONA AIRPORT

AIRPORT MESA

WEST SEDONA

CHOCLATREE

PICAZZO'S

COFFEE POT RESTAURANT

DAHL & DI LUCA RISTORANTE

CAFÉ JOSE

WILD ORCHID

BARKING FROG GRILLE

89A

THAI SPICES

To JEROME, RED ROCK CROSSING, Red Rock State Park, Tuzigoot National Monument, and Dead Horse Ranch State Park

0.5 mi

0.5 km

© AVALON TRAVEL

Uptown Sedona's shops and galleries, with Snoopy Rock in the background

temperatures are mild, spring wildflowers or autumn leaves are added incentives. Summer, on the other hand, is hot, with highs in the mid- to high-90s, though it cools off considerably at night. The occasional dusting of snow—along with annual holiday lights and hotel bargains—make a winter trip an intriguing option.

HISTORY

To first-time visitors, Sedona may appear to be a newly inhabited boomtown. Sure, its red buttes are millions of years old, but the freshly stuccoed shopping centers and recently constructed housing developments don't inspire a sense of history. The truth is, though, people have been coming to Sedona and the Verde Valley for thousands of years, lured by the dramatic surroundings, rich natural resources, and mild climate.

The Sinagua were the first to leave a lasting mark on the area. Sometime during the first millennium, they began raising crops. They built pit houses dating to A.D. 650, and later moved to cliff dwellings and hilltop pueblos. Sinagua ruins can be found throughout Red Rock Country and the Verde Valley, including the stunning Montezuma Castle, all abandoned by 1400. Archaeologists believe many Sinagua families joined other Ancestral Puebloans to the north, while some stayed behind and joined the seminomadic Yavapai bands who entered the area around A.D. 1300.

In 1876, after Yavapais and Apaches were forced onto reservations by the U.S. government, J. J. Thompson arrived in Oak Creek Canyon, settling on a piece of land where Indian crops still grew and calling it Indian Gardens. Additional ranching and farming families moved into the area, including T. C. Schnebly, an entrepreneurial settler who built a two-story wood-frame house where Tlaquepaque and the Los Abrigados Resort now stand. Schnebly ran a general store, lodged

THE MOVIES COME TO SEDONA

In 1923 five army trucks loaded with equipment slowly made their way down the switchbacks of Oak Creek Canyon to West Fork. Hollywood had arrived.

Call of the Canyon, based on a Zane Grey novel, was the first of more than 80 movies that would be made in the Sedona area, many filmed during the golden age of westerns. Among the finest are *Angel and the Badman* (1946), *Broken Arrow* (1950), and *The Rounders* (1965). The latter is notable not only for being a good flick, but also because it was the first film in which Sedona played itself. Until then, Sedona stood in for Canada (*Pony Soldier,* 1952), Bisbee (*3:10 to Yuma,* 1957), southeastern Arizona's Apache country (*Broken Arrow,* 1950), and other locales.

Hosting Hollywood often required the cooperation and ingenuity of locals (who ironically didn't have a movie theater of their own until 1975). A town set was constructed in Grasshopper Flat (now West Sedona), and a soundstage once stood where a hotel is located today. For *Pony Soldier,* workers added ponderosa pines to make convincing backdrops for Canadian Mounties. Wax saguaros decorated the set of *Broken Arrow,* one of many films that lives on in Sedona's place-names, which include streets called Gun Fury, Fabulous Texan, and Johnny Guitar.

Among the actors who worked in the red rocks: William Boyd (Hopalong Cassidy), Errol Flynn, John Wayne, Barbara Stanwyck, Burt Lancaster, Robert Mitchum, Hedy Lamarr, Jane Russell, James Stewart, Glenn Ford, Henry Fonda, Joan Crawford, Rock Hudson, Yvonne DeCarlo, Richard Widmark, Elvis Presley, Woody Harrelson, Robert De Niro, and Johnny Depp. A local history buff with plans to establish a film museum has put together a list of movies made in the Sedona area (www.arizonaslittleholly-wood.com).

You can also learn more about the local film résumé at the **Sedona Heritage Museum,** and your hotel room might have a few DVDs for loan. If you're a true-blue movie buff, check out the **Yavapai College film school** (928/649-4276, www.yc.edu), or visit in February for the annual film festival (www.sedonafilmfestival.com). During the weeklong event, more than 150 films are screened, from student shorts to indie flicks to Hollywood features.

guests, and established the area's first post office in 1902, which required him to submit a name for the burgeoning community. After the postmaster general in Washington rejected Schnebly Station and Oak Creek Crossing as being too long for a cancellation stamp, Schnebly followed his brother's advice and submitted his wife's name, Sedona.

In the early 1900s, more settlers began to stream into the Verde Valley, where they found work as farmers or in Jerome's ore-rich mines. However, it was another industry that would make Sedona famous: the movies. Hollywood filmed many of its classic westerns against the backdrop of Sedona's massive rock formations, beginning with Zane Grey's *Call of the Canyon* in 1923. Since then, stars from John Wayne to Johnny Depp have shot nearly a hundred movies and TV episodes in the area, and the rugged terrain continues to attract filmmakers.

Sedona's tourism industry took off as Americans began to explore the country by car after WWII. In the 1980s and 1990s, Sedona boomed as a retirement and vacation destination. More than half of the land around Sedona has been protected by state parks and national forest, driving up real estate values and pushing many new residents into neighboring areas, such as the Village of Oak Creek and Cottonwood. Still, some 11,000 people live in Sedona today—outnumbered by 3.5 million visitors every year—and the community manages to retain plenty of small-town character.

Sights

Sedona's main attraction is its awe-inspiring landscape. Reddish sandstone buttes, blue skies, and evergreen junipers and piñons dominate the horizon, while refreshing Oak Creek cuts through town, creating a peaceful, leafy axis. Make driving scenic byways and hiking the numerous trails your top priorities, but set aside some time to visit Chapel of the Holy Cross or other attractions before losing yourself in the plethora of shops and galleries.

UPTOWN AND HIGHWAY 179
◖ Chapel of the Holy Cross

In a region of such natural beauty, it's hard for a man-made structure not to compete or detract, which is why the Chapel of the Holy Cross (780 Chapel Rd., 928/282-4069, www.chapeloftheholycross.com, 9 A.M.–5 P.M. Mon.–Sat., 10 A.M.–5 P.M. Sun., free) is such

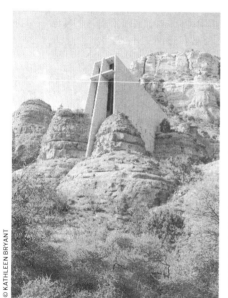

© KATHLEEN BRYANT

Chapel of the Holy Cross

a treasure. Perched above neighborhood and forest, the Modernist chapel has a structural support that doubles as its central motif, a 90-foot-tall cross rising between two red sandstone outcroppings. Set amid a deep red layer of stone, a spiraling ramp gives visitors time to appreciate the site's very special ambience and panoramic views before entering the chapel.

The interior is embellished only by floor-to-ceiling windows framing red rocks and blue skies. The chapel's designer, Marguerite Brunswig Staude, wanted it to be a place of prayer, and an aura of peace permeates the simple interior, lit by flickering votives. Spend some quiet time here before visiting the small gift shop downstairs.

Staude's design was inspired by a 1932 trip to New York City, where she saw a cross in the steel-and-glass facade of the recently constructed Empire State Building. Early sketches of her glass cathedral impressed Lloyd Wright, son of architect Frank Lloyd Wright, but the archbishop of Los Angeles ultimately rejected them for a proposed cathedral. When Staude and her husband bought a ranch in Sedona in 1941, she found the perfect setting for her vision. The small chapel was completed in 1956.

Schnebly Hill Road

At the roundabout intersection on the south side of Oak Creek Bridge, you'll see a turn-off for Schnebly Hill Road, one of the most scenic—and rockiest—drives in Sedona. Take the time to travel the first mile, which is paved all the way to the **Schnebly Hill Trailhead,** where you'll find lots of parking and a few shaded picnic tables with postcard-pretty views of Uptown. Look across the road to see **Snoopy Rock** and **Camel Head.**

Linger to soak up the views or, if you have time and a high-clearance, four-wheel-drive vehicle, continue up Schnebly Hill Road. It's another bone-rattling five miles to Schnebly Hill Vista, a dirt parking area that makes a good turnaround point. En route you'll pass the softly rounded red sandstone buttes known as **The Cowpies** and **The Merry-Go-Round,** a red sandstone formation circled by blocks of gray limestone that make up the carousel "horses." (If you'd prefer not to risk your oil pan or suspension, you can make this trip on a guided Jeep tour.)

Institute of Ecotourism

Located next to the Tlaquepaque Arts and Crafts Village, the Institute of Ecotourism (91 Portal Ln., 928/282-2720, www.ioet.org, 10 A.M.–6 P.M. Mon.–Fri., free) introduces the region's natural history and indigenous cultures through interactive exhibits highlighting geology, astronomy, and Arizona's fragile ecosystem. The modest grounds showcase native plants, and weekly classes range from geology talks to botanical walks. More than a museum, this nonprofit serves as a think tank for environmentally sensitive travel and tourism.

Sedona Heritage Museum

Get a glimpse of how Sedona's pioneers lived at the Sedona Heritage Museum and Jordan Park (735 Jordan Rd., 928/282-7038, www.sedonamuseum.org, 11 A.M.–3 P.M. daily, $7 adults, $2 children), the former home and orchards of Walter and Ruth Jordan. The Jordans' original one-room cabin, built in 1930 from red rock, was expanded over the years to accommodate a growing family and business. Rooms are filled with photos and artifacts showing life in early Sedona, from the rough work of real cowboys to the Hollywood version. More than 80 movies were filmed in the area, many shot during Hollywood's golden age of westerns. Be sure to enjoy the grounds of the museum, encompassing a botanical walk, heritage apple trees, and the shed that houses vintage machinery, including Walter Jordan's apple sorter.

Sedona Arts Center

Launched in 1958 as a place for local artists to teach and share ideas, the Sedona Arts Center (15 Art Barn Rd., 928/282-3809, www.sedonaartscenter.com, 10 A.M.–5 P.M. daily) helped establish Sedona's reputation as an art town. SAC's galleries feature rotating exhibitions of work by local and regional artists, and the gift shop has an excellent selection of reasonably priced work, including fine art, jewelry, sculpture, pottery, textiles, and photography. An integral part of the community since its beginnings in George Jordan's old apple barn (now a gallery), SAC hosts receptions and events, including **First Friday Art Walks** and the annual **Plein Air Festival** held in October. Its Nassan Gobran School of the Arts offers more than a hundred art classes every year, including three- to five-day intensive art workshops and field expeditions.

WEST SEDONA
◖ Airport Mesa

For a breathtaking bird's-eye view of the city, drive Airport Road to the top of the mesa and **Airport Vista.** Walk across the road from the large parking area to the vista's paved overlook for sweeping views from Cockscomb on the west to Wilson Mountain on the east. See if you can identify Chimney Rock, Lizard Head, Capitol Butte, Sugar Loaf, Coffeepot Rock, and other formations by their shapes. As you might guess, this is a popular spot to watch a sunset. Past the vista, the airport and its mile-long landing strip host a number of plane and helicopter touring companies. You'll also find a hotel and restaurant.

As you drove up the mesa, you likely noticed a small pullout with room for a half-dozen cars on the left side of Airport Road. This is the start of a short scramble up to a rocky saddle, said to be the location of the **Airport vortex.** The saddle has beautiful views eastward to the cliffs that mark the edge of Munds Mountain.

Amitabha Stupa and Peace Park

Designed and constructed by the Buddhist group Kunzang Palyul Chöling (KPC), the 36-foot-tall Amitabha Stupa (2650 Pueblo Dr., 877/788-7229, www.stupas.org, dusk to dawn daily, free) graces 14 acres of piñon-juniper woodland below Chimney Rock. Tucked into a West Sedona neighborhood, this peaceful sanctuary receives about 20,000 visitors a year. Stupa architecture incorporates sacred symbols and numbers, and this stupa (dedicated to the Buddha of Compassion) was filled with thousands of prayers and offerings during its construction. Along winding footpaths, you will also see fluttering prayer flags, a smaller White Tara stupa, and a large carved wooden Buddha. Circumambulate the stupas, find a quiet spot for contemplation or meditation, or simply enjoy the views. KPC has continued to welcome the public to the stupa park, despite financial setbacks that may affect its future. To

get to the stupa park from State Route 89A, turn north on Andante Drive (at the Circle K) and continue for about a mile to Pueblo Drive. Turn left and proceed about 50 yards to the entrance, parking on the shoulder. Be respectful of private property as you walk the gently sloping path to the stupa.

◖ Red Rock Crossing

The view of **Cathedral Rock** from Oak Creek's Red Rock Crossing is said to be one of the most-photographed scenes in Arizona. Find it by taking State Route 89A west of town and turning left (south) on Upper Red Rock Loop Road. On its winding descent, the narrow paved road delivers tantalizing views of your destination. Turn left again at Chavez Ranch Road, then follow signs for Red Rock Crossing and **Crescent Moon Recreation Area** (928/203-2900, www.fs.fed.us/r3/Coconino, 8 A.M.–8 P.M. daily Memorial Day–Labor Day, otherwise closing at dusk, $9 per vehicle). This is a popular spot for weddings, picnics, and especially for photographers, thanks to the cool waters of Oak Creek and postcard views of Cathedral Rock's spires, perhaps the loveliest of Sedona's famed vortex sites. Informal paths meander along the creek to swimming holes like Buddha Beach, where visitants pile improbable stacks of rocks. You can also arrive at this lovely spot on foot or mountain bike via the Templeton Trail, which starts at the Back O' Beyond trailhead (off State Route 179). Or, from the Village of Oak Creek, drive to the end of the Verde Valley School Road and cross the creek on foot. (If the simple plank bridge has washed away, you'll find plenty of stepping stones.)

Red Rock State Park

Oak Creek flows through 286-acre Red Rock State Park (4050 Red Rock Loop Rd., 928/282-6907, http://azstateparks.com/parks/rero, 8 A.M.–5 P.M. daily, $6 per vehicle), the

© KATHLEEN BRYANT

The Amitabha Stupa and Peace Park are situated below Chimney Rock.

SEEING RED

The red rocks' famous color is just one small chapter in a complex geological story. The dramatic and vibrant landscape was created over eons, as this part of Arizona has been submerged by seas, alternated between muddy coastal plain and Sahara-like dunes, and endured volcanic eruptions, leaving behind colorful layers of limestone, sandstone, and basalt.

These layers are exposed at the edge of the massive, uplifted Colorado Plateau, which extends well into the Four Corners region. The plateau's exposed southern edge—known as the Mogollon Rim—has eroded into fantastically sculpted buttes and tall, slender spires. From the ground up, you'll see deep red Hermit shale; the 700-foot-thick horizontally banded Schnebly Hill formation; the aeolian (wind-deposited) light-gold Coconino sandstone; and on the highest peaks, the almost-white Kaibab limestone. In places, a cap of hard basalt (cooled lava), protects the softer layers underneath.

And the varying shades of red? Dissolved, oxidized iron—more prosaically known as rust—has permeated the sedimentary sandstone layers. Those who want to learn more about Sedona's geological history will find intriguing interpretive displays at Red Rock State Park and the forest service's Red Rock Visitor Center.

© KATHLEEN BRYANT

Sandstone rock layers have eroded into fantastic forms.

site of some of the area's earliest homesteads. Opened in 1991, the park serves as a protected riparian habitat for native wildlife and plants, as well as hosting an environmental education center (9 A.M.–5 P.M. daily) with interactive exhibits and a small theater. Architectural features include a viewing patio and a geology wall made up of the various layers of sandstone, limestone, and basalt from Sedona's famed rock formations. Volunteers and naturalists lead bird walks and nature hikes, including monthly full moon walks. The park's half-dozen short trails can be linked for longer hikes. To get to the park, take Upper or Lower Red Rock Loop Road off State Route 89A and follow the signs.

Prehistoric Ruins and Rock Art

About 15 miles northwest of town, **Palatki** (928/282-3854, 9 A.M.–3 P.M. daily, $5 per vehicle, reservations recommended) is a red-rock cliff dwelling occupied by Sinagua villagers eight hundred years ago. A short trail leads to **Red Cliffs,** a series of alcoves holding more than 5,000 pictographs and petroglyphs. To get here, take State Route 89A eight miles west of the Y intersection. Just past mile marker 365, turn right on Forest Road 525, a good dirt road suitable for most passenger cars when conditions are dry. Drive five miles to a fork; stay right, continuing on Forest Road 795 to the parking lot. After touring Palatki, you can make a scenic loop back to Sedona by turning left (east) on the Boynton Pass Road (Forest Road 152C), which changes from a rough dirt road to pavement after a couple miles. Continue to a "T," where you'll turn right, and then right again at the next "T" onto Dry Creek Road, which will return you to West Sedona.

If you have a sturdy vehicle, you can venture even farther into the cliffs and canyons to visit **Honanki** (10 A.M.–6 P.M. daily, weather permitting). This prehistoric village and rock art site tucked below Loy Butte is four miles away from Palatki via Forest Road 525. It's a good idea to check first with the forest service (928/203-7500) or the rangers at Palatki (928/282-3854) for directions and current road conditions, and your parking pass for Palatki is good for Honanki as well. Alternatively, you can travel to Honanki via a Pink Jeep tour.

VILLAGE OF OAK CREEK
Ranger Station and Visitor Center

The Red Rock Ranger District's **Visitor Center** (8375 State Route 179, 928/203-7500, 8 A.M.–5 P.M. daily), located just south of the Village of Oak Creek, has exhibits and a small retail area with fun nature-themed gifts, as well as books and maps. The expansive veranda out front is a great spot to snap a panoramic shot of Bell Rock and Courthouse Butte. You can ask for information about trails and scenic drives, and pick up a **Red Rock Pass** ($5 day, $15/week), required for parking at some forest service trailheads.

Scenic Red Rock Byway

Much of State Route 179 is designated as the Scenic Red Rock Byway, and it's easy to understand why. Rocky monuments line both sides of the road, luring you deeper into Red Rock Country. Paved pullouts and parking areas provide a safe place to stop and admire the views or take photos. After passing through VOC's main drag, look right (east) for the **Bell Rock Vista** parking area, a picnic spot and hub for biking and hiking trails. You'll easily recognize **Bell Rock.** Just east of the bell-shaped butte, is blocky **Courthouse Butte** and, across the highway to the west, **Castle Rock.**

As you continue toward Sedona on State Route 179, you'll pass **Cathedral Rock** (which from this side looks a little like a natural reddish Stonehenge), the **Little Horse** trailhead and parking area, and the Chapel of the Holy Cross, rising out of the red rocks near the spires known as **The Nuns** and the **Madonna and Child.** The scenic road designation ends at milepost 310, but the stunning views continue.

V-Bar-V Heritage Site

Archaeology buffs will be intrigued by the large rock art panel at V-Bar-V (9:30 A.M.–3 P.M. Fri.–Mon.), a former ranch along Beaver Creek. Now a heritage site under the protection of the forest service, it boasts the densest concentration of petroglyphs (rock art pecked into stone) in the area, including a possible solar calendar. To get here, take State Route 179 south of the Village of Oak Creek toward I-17. Continue under the freeway, where the road becomes Forest Road 618. It's three paved miles to the parking lot and a short (0.3 mile) stroll to the site, where docents share their knowledge of the Sinagua culture.

Entertainment and Events

Sedona hosts a handful of notable festivals and events, most crowding the calendar in spring and fall. Yet, despite the millions of tourists who visit annually, this is still a small town, with a slow pace and relaxed atmosphere that mean you won't discover a buzzing club scene. A number of local restaurants host local musicians during evening hours, and there are live performances around town most every weekend. But you may find that a quiet night under the stars is just the right way to cap a full day of hiking and exploring the red rocks.

NIGHTLIFE

Couples will find plenty of romantic restaurants in which to enjoy a glass of wine, and the big resorts expertly set the mood with cozy fireplaces and leafy patios. Make the 15-minute drive to **Enchantment Resort** (525 Boynton Canyon Rd., 928/282-2900, http://enchantmentresort.com), which is nestled in the horseshoe-shaped Boynton Canyon. The red-rock walls glow at sunset and provide a memorable backdrop for a drink in the lounge, where glass walls unfold to take in the view. The creekside bar at **L'Auberge de Sedona** (301 L'Auberge Ln., 928/282-1661, www.lauberge.com) in Uptown Sedona is an intimate, alfresco spot to share a bottle of wine.

If you want to catch a game on TV, **Stakes and Sticks Sports Bar and Grill** (160 Portal Ln., 928/204-7849, 11 A.M.–11 P.M. daily) at Los Abrigados Resort has two dozen screens broadcasting the wide world of sports. True to its promise of "pilsner, pool, and ponies," here you can wager on horse races at the automated betting stations inside the billiards room or enjoy a beer on the more subdued patio.

The **Rooftop Cantina** (321 N. State Route 89A, 928/282-4179, 11 A.M.–9 P.M. daily) at Oaxaca Restaurant has a menu of 50 tequilas that can be mixed into some tasty margaritas. The views of Snoopy Rock are as much fun as the atmosphere at this Uptown Mexican restaurant.

Live music is on the menu most nights at **Sound Bites Grill** (101 N. State Route 89A, 928/282-2713, www.soundbitesgrille.com, 11 A.M.–11 P.M. Tues.–Sun., till midnight Fri.–Sat.) in Uptown's Piñon Pointe shops. The owners have a sister establishment in the VOC, the **Marketplace Café** (6645 State Route 179, 928/284-5478, www.mpcsedona.com, 11 A.M.–9 P.M. Sun.–Thurs., till 10 P.M. Fri.–Sat.), where you're likely to find live music on weekends.

Join the friendly crowd and casual vibe at **Full Moon Saloon** (7000 State Route 179, 928/284-1872, www.thefullmoonsaloon.com, 11 A.M.–2 A.M. daily) at Tequa Marketplace in the Village of Oak Creek. Depending on when you drop by, you might find a pool tournament, karaoke, open mic, or the occasional live band.

PJ's Village Pub & Sports Lounge (40 W. Cortez Dr., 928/284-2250, www.pjsvillagepub.com, 10 A.M.–2 A.M. daily) is another laid-back watering hole in the Village of Oak Creek that packs in locals with live music on Saturday nights. You'll find regulars playing darts and video games, as well as three pool tables that are free on Sunday evenings.

Olde Sedona Bar & Grill (1405 W. State Route 89A, 928/282-5670, www.oldesedona.com, 11 A.M.–2 A.M. daily) in West Sedona offers live entertainment most nights. The second-story patio has a view of the red rocks, or head downstairs to the bar, where you can dance, shoot pool, or shoot the breeze with new friends.

During temperate months, musicians take to the outdoor stage next to the **Martini Bar**

(1350 W. State Route 89A, 928/282-9288, 3 P.M.–2 A.M. daily). The pond-centered patio makes a pleasant gathering spot in West Sedona, with entertainment most nights between 7 and 10 P.M.

West Sedona's **Oak Creek Brewing Company** (2050 Yavapai Rd., 928/203-9441, www.oakcreekbrew.com, 4–11 P.M. Mon.–Thurs., noon–1 A.M. Fri.–Sun.) serves up award-winning craft beers, like its popular amber ale and refreshing hefeweizen. Take a seat near the fermentation tanks or head out to the patio to listen to live music, which ranges from Celtic and rockabilly to a weekly drumming circle. You can soak up your brew with a hot dog, but if you're hungry for a full meal, the brewery's more upscale grill is located in Tlaquepaque.

You never know what you'll find at **Relics Restaurant & Lounge at Rainbow's End** (3235 W. State Route 89A, 928/282-1593, www.relicsrestaurant.com, 4 P.M.–2 A.M. daily), a former homestead, USO club, and roller rink. The dancehall retains much of its rustic ambience, boasting northern Arizona's largest wooden dance floor and hosting weekly events, including 1950s revues, Latino nights, and DJ dance parties that range from Motown to country. If the barroom looks a little familiar, you may have seen it in *The Rounders* (1965), a Western comedy starring Henry Fonda and Glenn Ford.

PERFORMING ARTS

Canyon Moon Theatre Company (6601 State Route 179, 928/282-6212, www.canyonmoontheatre.org) stages a mix of dramas, comedies, and musicals at its theater in the Village of Oak Creek. **Shakespeare Sedona** (602/535-1202, www.swshakespeare.org) performs on select summer evenings in the courtyards of Tlaquepaque.

Chamber Music Sedona (928/204-2415, www.chambermusicsedona.org) presents an eclectic series of artists year-round at venues throughout Sedona, from pianists and string quartets to Latin guitar and small jazz bands. Check the website for performance dates and locations.

In West Sedona, **Studio Live** and **the Backyard** (215 Coffeepot Dr., 928/282-0549, www.studiolivesedona.com) host weekly performances by indie musicians, with recent appearances by Patty Larkin, Maria Muldaur, and Stanley Jordan. Home to the Sedona Performing Arts Alliance, this is also a great place to catch community events like theme nights and songwriter showcases.

The **Mary D. Fisher Theater** (2030 W. State Route 89A, 928/282-1177, www.sedonafilmfestival.com) is a small jewel, screening independent and foreign films every week, with occasional treats like big-screen, hi-def performances from London's National Theater or programs such as *Live from NY's 92nd Street Y*.

"New Age" is a convenient and somewhat inaccurate label for a host of performances, lectures, and events appealing to local residents, spiritual pilgrims, travel gypsies, and global music fans, held at various venues around town. You might, for example, watch a belly dance troupe at a local restaurant, attend an astrology lecture at the Unity church (65 Deertail Dr., 928/282-7181, www.unityofsedona.com), or sing along with a touring kirtan musician at 7 Centers Yoga Arts (2115 Mountain Rd., 928/203-4400, www.7centers.com). Self-improvement gurus and spiritual leaders like Deepak Chopra, Wayne Dyer, Ram Dass, Don Miguel Ruiz, Julia Cameron have visited Sedona, many of them appearing at the **Sedona Creative Life Center** (333 Schnebly Hill Rd., 928/282-9300, www.sedonacreativelifecenter.com), situated on a lovely 15-acre site near Oak Creek. Large community events and concerts are held in Posse Grounds Park or the Performing Arts Center at Red Rock High School.

For information about current happenings, stop by the Chamber of Commerce Visitor Center (1 Forest Rd., 928/282-7722 or 800/288-7336, www.visitsedona.com, 8:30 A.M.–5 P.M. Mon.–Sat., 8 A.M.–3 P.M. Sun.) or look for flyers at community bulletin boards in local bookstores and restaurants. Or pick up a free copy of *Kudos,* a weekly newspaper with the latest entertainment listings.

FESTIVALS AND EVENTS

Sedona's cultural calendar encompasses everything from intimate studio tours to grand galas. Most large outdoor events are scheduled for fall, when the weather is at its finest. To find out more about upcoming events, check

SEDONA'S ARTISTIC TRADITION

See an exhibit, take a class, or shop at the gallery at Sedona Arts Center.

It's no surprise why so many artists follow their muse to Sedona. The sculptural rock forms and bold color palette are powerful inspiration. Over the decades, a growing artistic community has helped shape the town and define its identity. Among the first to arrive were surrealist Max Ernst, who lived here briefly in the 1940s; painter Stephen Juharos, who opened Treasure Art Gallery; and Egyptian émigré and sculptor Nassan Gobran, who arrived to teach at Verde Valley School. The burgeoning art scene really began to

take hold in 1958, when Gobran and other artists established an art school at the Jordans' apple and peach packing barn in Uptown Sedona. This studio/exhibition space evolved into the **Sedona Arts Center (SAC).** Today SAC continues its mission to serve as a resource for local artists, providing gallery and classroom space, and hosting festivals and events.

One of SAC's founding members, jeweler and sculptor Marguerite Brunswig Staude, gave Sedona its most iconic landmark in 1956, the Chapel of the Holy Cross. SAC also displays work by member Joe Beeler, a painter and sculptor who moved to Sedona in the early 1960s. In 1965, Beeler met with Charlie Dye, George Phippen, and John Hampton at the Oak Creek Tavern (now the Cowboy Club Grille & Spirits), where they formed the Cowboy Artists of America. Beeler died in 2006, after seeing CAA grow into a respected organization whose members' works are prized by collectors.

As you explore Sedona's artistic side, you'll find numerous public sculptures, dozens of galleries, and top-notch events like the **Sedona Arts Festival** (www.sedonaartsfestival.org) and the **Plein Air Festival** (www.sedonapleinairfestival. com). Little wonder Sedona was named one of America's best small art towns by *American Style* magazine.

To immerse yourself in the local art scene, join the **First Friday** art walk, when galleries host receptions and artist demonstrations from 5 to 8 P.M. The Sedona Trolley offers free transportation between galleries. For more information, contact the **Sedona Gallery Association** (928/282-7390, www.sedonagalleryassociation.com).

© KATHLEEN BRYANT

the Sedona Events Alliance calendar (www.sedonaeventsalliance.org).

Spring

March is Arizona's Archaeology and Heritage Awareness Month, with dozens of events throughout the state. One, V-Bar-V Ranch's **Archaeology Discovery Days** (www.azstateparks.com, 928/203-2909), showcases prehistoric technologies like flint-knapping. Traditional foods are available for sampling, and visitors can try their hand at throwing an atlatl (hunting spear) or weaving yucca fiber sandals.

Late in April, the **Verde Valley Birding and Nature Festival** (www.birdyverde.org) celebrates the region's diverse natural habitats. Affectionately dubbed the "Birdy Verde," the multiday event hosted by Cottonwood's Dead Horse Ranch State Park includes expert speakers, field trips, and workshops. Past programs have featured lectures about Sedona geology, river trips, guided bird walks, and kid-centric games and activities.

Tlaquepaque (www.tlaq.com) hosts events throughout the year, but one of the most colorful occurs on **Cinco de Mayo** weekend, when folklorico dancers, mariachi musicians, and a chili contest lend a street party atmosphere to the shopping village.

Summer

On the first weekend in June, the Chamber Music Sedona strikes a different note with its **Bluegrass Festival** (www.chambermusicsedona.org), featuring two days of finger-pickin' music, including workshops, a free community program, and an outdoor concert and barbecue.

The **Red Rock Music Festival** (877/733-7257, www.redrocksmusicfestival.com) in late August and early September attracts classical musical lovers for a vibrant showcase of chamber and orchestral music, as well as performances by flamenco and Native American performers. Concerts and events are held at venues throughout Sedona.

A long list of small-town celebrations (including the National Day of the Cowboy in July and the Moonlight Madness street festival marking Labor Day) are scheduled throughout summer, which is also the season for **open studio tours** hosted by members of the Sedona Visual Artists Coalition (http://sedonaartistscoalition.org).

Autumn

The answer to Sedona's increasingly commercial art scene is **Gumption Fest** (www.gumptionfest.org), when local and regional artists gather for a weekend of music, dance, art, and poetry, including the Haiku Death Match Poetry Slam. The free festival takes over a slice of West Sedona along Coffeepot Drive in mid-September.

In late September, the venerable **Sedona Jazz on the Rocks** (928/282-0590, www.sedonajazz.com) showcases live outdoor jazz performances. Spyro Gyra, Herbie Hancock, Diane Krall, and Poncho Sanchez have all taken the stage under the red rocks. In recent years, venues and dates have shifted; call or check the website for the current schedule.

In October, look for the sea of white tents near Red Rock High School marking the **Sedona Arts Festival** (995 Upper Red Rock Loop Rd., 928/204-9456, www.sedonaartsfestival.org), when more than 100 artists gather to show their work. There's also live music, food booths, and the Kid Zone, where children can create their own masterpieces.

The **Sedona Plein Air Festival** (928/282-3809, www.sedonapleinairfestival.com) in late October attracts artists from around the United States to paint "in the open air," a technique made famous by the French Impressionists. The weeklong event—at trailheads, creeks, and parks throughout town—includes demonstrations and workshops for painters hoping to develop their technical abilities, as well for art lovers who like to "brush up" their observation skills.

Winter

When the weather turns chilly in late November, more than a million lights go up at Los Abrigados Resort & Spa for **Red Rock Fantasy** (1090 W. State Route 89A, 928/282-1777, www.redrockfantasy.com). Participants compete by creating traditional and quirky nighttime displays that twinkle through the holiday season. In early December, neighboring Tlaquepaque hosts a Southwestern holiday tradition, the **Festival of Lights** (336 State Route 179, 928/282-4838, www.tlaq.com). Some 6,000 luminarias—small paper bags filled with sand and a single lit candle—glow in the shopping village's charming courtyards and stairways.

Runners converge the first week of February for the **Sedona Marathon** (800/775-7671, www.sedonamarathon.com). The challenging course, some of it on dirt forest roads, offers spectacular views and a few wildlife sightings as it wends its way from West Sedona to Boynton Pass. The full- and half-marathon runs, as well as the more manageable 5K option, are open to runners of all levels.

The last week of February, the **Sedona International Film Festival** (2030 W. State Route 89A, 928/282-1177, www.sedonafilm-festival.com) presents more than 100 movies from around the world, including big-budget features, documentaries, shorts, and student films. Workshops and parties round out the schedule, with directors, producers, and stars frequently in attendance.

Shopping

After admiring the red rocks, shopping is probably Sedona's most popular activity, with the vast majority of stores targeting the out-of-state visitors who flock here for a taste of Arizona—or to experience the New Age vibe. Specialty stores sell cactus jellies, cowboy boots and hats, colorful pottery, and mystical gemstones. You'll also find Native American arts and crafts from tiny carved fetishes to room-size Navajo rugs, and a thriving gallery scene that attracts serious collectors as well as first-time buyers.

UPTOWN AND HIGHWAY 179

Uptown boasts the greatest concentration of souvenir shops, clothing boutiques, and Western-themed galleries. Just south of Uptown along State Route 179, there's a pedestrian-friendly stretch of galleries ranging from mammoth, light-filled spaces selling large-format bronzes and canvases to intimate studios

specializing in handcrafted furniture, pottery, glass, or jewelry. On the **First Friday** of every month, galleries host receptions and stay open till 8 P.M.

Jewelry and Fashion

Looking for a piece of turquoise jewelry? Find this classic Southwestern stone at the **Turquoise Buffalo** (252 N. State Route 89A, 928/282-2994, www.turquoisebuffalo.com, 9 A.M.–6 P.M. Tues.–Wed., 9 A.M.–7:30 P.M. Thurs.–Mon.), which stocks more than 1,700 unique pieces. The helpful staff guides buyers and browsers through dozens of varieties of turquoise, from the green-veined Lone Mountain and the copper-flecked Morenci to the creamy white variations.

Also in Uptown, **Blue-Eyed Bear** (450 Jordan Rd., 928/282-9081, www.blueeyed-bear.com, 9 A.M.–5:30 P.M. daily) specializes in handmade pieces in sterling silver, gold, and semiprecious stones, all designed by Native American and Southwestern artists. The necklaces, bracelets, and earrings evoke Arizona's indigenous roots while the clean lines and bold colors give the work a modern feel.

A handful of shops sell fashions from local designers. At **Looking West** (242 N. State Route 89A, 928/282-4877, daily) you'll find clothing designed and made in Sedona—flowing "broomstick" skirts, comfortable jackets, and accessories. **Victorian Cowgirl** (181 State Route 179, 877/232-3455 or 928/282-0778, www.victoriancowgirl.com, 10 A.M.–6 P.M. daily) has become a popular choice for brides and other romantics, though steampunks would also fall for the beautifully tailored garments with turn-of-the-20th-century flair. Gentlemen, don't feel left out: Head for **Cowboy Corral** (219 N. State Route 89A, 928/282-2040, www.cowboycorral.com, 10 A.M.–6 P.M. daily) where wannabe desperados outfit themselves with dusters, vests, and handmade hats. Leather fashions are the specialty at **UpWest** (470 N. State Route 89A, 928/204-1341, www.upwestleather.com, 10 A.M.–5 P.M. daily), housed in the historic Jordan sales building, where Sedona's Depression-era farmers sold fruit.

For a well-dressed home and a peek at old Sedona, stop by the landmarked **Hummingbird House** (100 Brewer Rd., 928/282-0705, 10 A.M.–5 P.M. Mon.–Sat., 11:30 A.M.–3:30 P.M. Sun.). Tucked behind a white picket fence and shaded by large sycamore trees, the 1920s general store has been lovingly refurbished, complete with an old waterwheel that churns outside. It now sells collectible Americana and reproductions, furniture and garden decor, and exquisitely curated toiletries and gifts.

The Shops at Hyatt Piñon Pointe

On a small bluff overlooking the Y intersection of State Routes 179 and 89A, The Shops at Hyatt Piñon Pointe (101 N. State Route 89A, 928/254-1006, www.theshopsathyattpinonpointe.com) include some interesting independent boutiques along with a few chains, which are creeping into Sedona. **Marchesa's Fine Shoe Salon** (928/282-3212, 10 A.M.–6 P.M. daily) stocks heels, boots, and sandals by high-end designers like Marc Jacobs, Betsey Johnson, Christian LaCroix, and Stuart Weitzman, as well as more affordable options. **George Kelly Fine Jewelers** (928/282-8884, www.sedonafinejewelry.com, 10 A.M.–6 P.M. daily) carries imaginative and contemporary necklaces and rings. And for a tasty souvenir or gift, pick up a bottle of Arizona vino at **The Art of Wine** (877/903-9463, www.artowine.com, 10 A.M.–6 P.M. Mon.–Wed., 10 A.M.–8 P.M. Thurs.–Sun.).

◖ Tlaquepaque Arts and Crafts Village

Rarely does a shopping center become an attraction in its own right, but the charming Tlaquepaque (336 State Route 179, 928/282-4838, www.tlaq.com, shops open 10 A.M.–5 P.M. daily) is a beloved Sedona landmark. Even if you're not a shopper, come for one of Tlaquepaque's lively weekend festivals, or simply to enjoy the fountains and lushly landscaped courtyards. Its creator, Abe Miller, purchased a 4.5-acre garden business on the banks of Oak Creek in the early 1970s, promising the owners that he would do his best to preserve the site's sycamore trees. He envisioned an artists' enclave where visitors could see craftspeople at work. For inspiration, he visited Mexican towns and villages, including the original Tlaquepaque, an elegant colonial retreat outside of Guadalajara.

Miller replicated the colonial town's tile-embellished buildings, stairways, and courtyards, wrapping them around the old sycamore and catalpa trees, and incorporating truckloads of ironwork, carved doors, and other details he shipped north from Mexico. He was particularly proud of the chapel, a romanticized confection of stained-glass windows, hand-carved leather pews, and adobe walls. And though Miller's vision of a live-work artists' village proved unviable, Tlaquepaque (pronounced tuh-LAH-kuh-PAH-kee) is home to dozens of boutiques, galleries, cafés, and restaurants, including a few of the original tenants. Recent additions making room for larger enterprises were given a patina of age, so that old and new are almost indistinguishable.

Under the clock tower, **Rowe Gallery** (928/282-8877, www.rowegallery.com) displays distinguished Western bronzes and paintings. Sculptor and owner Ken Rowe is often on hand answering questions or demonstrating technique. (Rowe and Kim Kori, whose works are also in the gallery, created the large bronze ravens and eagle that grace the double roundabout at the Sedona's Y intersection.)

For a colorful collection of handblown glass art, visit **Kuivato Glass Gallery** (928/282-1212, www.kuivato.com). The delicate glass sculptures, fountains, and chandeliers sparkle in the light, tempting many buyers to ship one of the fragile pieces home. **Isadora** (928/282-6232) stocks hand-loomed coats and vests in bold patterns, as well as Native American–inspired shawls and scarves.

One of Tlaquepaque's original tenants, **Cocopah** (928/282-4928, www.beadofthemonthclub.com) bills itself the "oldest bead store in Arizona," and also carries an impressive array of Art Nouveau and Art Deco estate jewelry, antique Tibetan beads, and Native American jewelry and accessories. **Hyde Out Fine Leathers** (928/282-1292) sells handbags, jackets, luggage, and belts in buttery tans and browns, deep reds, and rich blacks.

The Garland Building

At the foot of Schnebly Hill Road, the red-rock Garland Building (411 State Route 179, 10 A.M.–5 P.M. Mon.–Sat., 11 A.M.–5 P.M. Sun.) is home to a handful of shops, including Mary Margaret's delightful **Sedona Pottery** (928/282-1192, http://sedonapotter.com); **Kopavi** (928/282-4774, http://kopaviinternational.com), specializing in Hopi jewelry; and **Garland's Navajo Rugs** (928/282-4070, www.garlandsrugs.com). For more than 30 years, the Garland family has purchased directly from Indian artists, amassing a vast selection of Navajo weavings, including antique pieces and hard-to-find large floor rugs. You'll also see tastefully displayed Navajo sand paintings, hand-carved Hopi kachina dolls, Pueblo pottery, and handwoven baskets.

Hozho

Santa Fe–style Hozho (431 State Route 179, 10 A.M.–5:30 P.M. Mon.–Sat., 11 A.M.–5 P.M. Sun.) hosts a diverse lineup. **Turquoise Tortoise Gallery** (928/282-2262, www.turqtortsedona.com) has sculpture, jewelry, and contemporary paintings by Tony Abeyta, David Johns, and other artists. **Lanning Gallery** (928/282-6865, www.lanninggallery.com) features classic and contemporary paintings, as well as ceramics, glass, and handmade furniture. You could say that **The Hike House** (928/282-5820, http://thehikehouse.com) specializes in the art of hiking—it's a great stop for picking up maps and gear or learning more about trails.

Hillside

Farther south on State Route 179, **Hillside Sedona** (671 State Route 179, 928/282-4500, www.hillsidesedona.net, 10 A.M.–6 P.M. daily) is home to restaurants, specialty shops, and galleries, including the long-running **James Ratliff Gallery** (928/282-1404, www.jamesratliffgallery.com, 10 A.M.–5 P.M. Mon.–Sat., 11 A.M.–5 P.M. Sun.), selling high-end bronzes and strikingly modern Southwestern canvases. **El Prado** (928/282-7309, www.elpradogalleries.com) showcases contemporary and Western paintings (including John Cogan's Grand Canyon scenes), but it's perhaps best known for large metal sculptures that twist and revolve in the wind.

WEST SEDONA

West of the Y along State Route 89A, mostly residential West Sedona is home to service businesses like grocers and hardware stores, though newer hotels have spurred more shops catering to visitors. The interests of locals and visitors intersect at the plethora of metaphysical shops selling books, crystals, and gifts.

New Age

Explore Sedona's New Age side at **Crystal Magic** (2978 W. State Route 89A, 928/282-1622, www.crystalmagicsedona.com, 9 A.M.–9 P.M. Mon.–Sat., 9 A.M.–8 P.M. Sun.), "a resource center for discovery and personal growth." Take home some healing crystals or stock up on aromatherapy oils and candles, feng shui supplies, incense, books, or music. The store also serves as an unofficial chamber of commerce where you can find information about metaphysical events and services like psychic readings or reflexology. Next door, the staff at **Magic Clothing** (2970 W. State Route 89A, 928/203-0053) can help you put together the gypsy goddess look popular in Sedona.

Mystical Bazaar (1449 W. State Route 89A, 928/204-5615, www.mysticalbazaar.com, 9 A.M.–8 P.M. Sun.–Wed., 9 A.M.–9 P.M. Thurs.–Sat.) sells jewelry made in Sedona, as well as a host of metaphysical items, including books, music, tarot cards, and crystals. The shop also offers aura photographs, which come with a 23-page report, and "facilitated spiritual tours" ranging from treks to Sedona's vortex spots to personalized shamanic journeys and starlight fire ceremonies.

Books

Owned by mystery author Kris Neri, the **Well Red Coyote** (3190 W. State Route 89A, 928/282-2284, www.wellredcoyote.com, 10 A.M.–6 P.M. Mon.–Sat.) stocks general interest books as well as regional titles, and often hosts weekend author events, poetry readings, and live musical performances.

Arts and Crafts

Raven's Nest (1145 W. State Route 89A, 928/204-2728, www.ravensnest-silversmith.com, 10 A.M.–5 P.M. Mon.–Sat., 1–5 P.M. Sun.), housed in a circular building at the corner of Airport Road, is a treasure trove of old pawn (items that were pawned for cash and not redeemed, once a common practice on Southwest reservations). Owner and silversmith Bob Colony is usually on hand for advice and repairs. The store also sells contemporary Native American jewelry, photographic art, and a selection of handmade gift items.

Mexidona (1670 W. State Route 89A, 928/282-0858, www.mexidona.com, 10 A.M.–5 P.M. daily) imports furniture, architectural embellishments, and handcrafted decor from Mexico, including Talavera, Mata Ortiz, and Oaxacan pottery.

Kachina House (2920 Hopi Dr., 928/204-9750, www.kachinahouse.com, 8:30 A.M.–4:30 P.M. Mon.–Fri., 8:30 A.M.–2:30 P.M. Sat., 10 A.M.–2 P.M. Sun.) is Arizona's largest distributor of Native American arts and crafts—many for reasonable prices. The 5,000-square-foot showroom sells hundreds of kachina dolls, ceremonial masks, horsehair pottery pieces, Hopi baskets, and sand paintings.

At the **Art Mart of Sedona** (2081 W. State Route 89A, 928/203-4576), located next to the Harkins movie theater, you'll find booth spaces offering a variety of arts and crafts, from inexpensive imported clothing to exquisite kachina figures carved and painted by local artist Gerald Quotskuyua.

VILLAGE OF OAK CREEK

Wonderfully unique shops have a habit of popping up in the Village, then fading away. Several of the big retail chains that were once a staple at the **Factory Outlet Mall** (6645 State Route 179, 10 A.M.–6 P.M. daily) have bowed out, but that's made room for interesting local shops like **The Worm** (928/282-3471, www.sedonaworm.com), which has the area's best selection of Southwestern books, as well as general titles, music, and gifts.

Buddha's Dream (51 Bell Rock Plaza, 928/554-4677, www.buddhasdreamllc.com, 10 A.M.–7 P.M. daily) is a must-stop for tea-drinkers. Not only does the shop carry a wide selection of organic teas, it also hosts free daily tastings and tea ceremony classes. Shop for books and handmade silk clothing, or inquire about the owner's traditional Chinese wedding-planning services.

Sports and Recreation

If you're not content viewing Sedona's majestic red rocks from the comfort of a hotel balcony or a restaurant patio, you'll find plenty of ways to get outside and get a little dirty. Hikers and bikers could spend weeks, if not months, exploring the miles and miles of trails that wind through the national forest, three wilderness areas, and two state parks. The diversity of topography and wildlife frequently surprises visitors.

Jeep tours over rugged forest roads hint at how the pioneers who arrived by stagecoach more than a century ago must have felt. Of course, there are more refined ways to sneak in your time outdoors: a round of golf, an alfresco massage at a four-star spa, or a hot-air balloon trip. No matter what you choose—guided hikes, biplane tours, river floats—be sure to wear sturdy shoes, a hat, and sunscreen when you venture outside. Also bring water—lots of it—as it's not uncommon to dehydrate quickly in this arid climate and moderate elevation.

TOURS
Jeep Tours

Taking a ride with iconic **Pink Jeep Tours** (204 N. State Route 89A, 928/282-5000, www.pinkjeep.com) is a popular way to romp over Sedona's red rocks. Entertaining guides describe the geology and ecosystem surrounding Sedona as they drive beefed-up Jeep Wranglers over steep boulders and occasionally treacherous passes. The popular Broken Arrow Tour ($75 adults, $56.25 children) explores Submarine Rock and scouts out postcard-perfect views from Chicken Point. The three-hour Ancient Ruins Tour ($72 adults, $54 children) stops at the ancient Sinagua cliff dwelling of Honanki and tracks down prehistoric rock art. Plush motorcoach tours to the Grand Canyon are also available ($125 adults, $115 children). Advanced reservations are recommended, though walk-ins can frequently get same-day seats.

Red Rock Western Jeep Tours (270 N. State Route 89A, Ste. 2, 928/282-6826, www.redrockjeep.com) offers four-wheeling excursions and much more. The cowboy guides may look like movie set extras, but these local experts enrich a traveler's understanding of Sedona's complex geology and wildlife. Red Rock's various outings range from romps with wine tasting to romantic private tours *à deux* to Western-themed treks that trace Apache and cowboy trails. The company also provides horseback riding, ranch cookouts, and sunset trips to the Grand Canyon. Basic Jeep tours

© KATHLEEN BRYANT

Jeep tours explore forest roads, vortex sites, and prehistoric ruins.

start around $50 per person. Parties of 10 or more may qualify for group rates.

If you're looking for a Jeep tour with a metaphysical approach, the guides at **Earth Wisdom Tours** (293 N. State Route 89A, 928/282-4714, www.earthwisdomtours.com) specialize in journeys that foster a deeper connection to the landscape and an appreciation for Native American spirituality. They'll take you on your choice of vortex tours, scenic drives, or hikes, all while imparting fascinating cultural and natural history. Two-hour tours start at $50 for adults; $25 for children under 12.

Adventure Tours

If you're not content letting the scenery pass you by from the seat of a Jeep, **Sedona Adventure Tours** (877/673-3661, www.sedonaadventure-tours.com) leads trips that highlight the area's diverse outdoor activities, including hiking, kayaking, and water tubing. The Water to Wine Tour ($130 adults) combines a four-mile

guided kayaking trip down the Verde River with a tour to Alcantara Vineyard for a pleasant afternoon of wine-tasting.

Adventures Out West (441 Forest Rd., 928/282-4611, www.advoutwest.com) offers Segway tours through Uptown or to the Chapel of the Holy Cross, starting at $65 and lasting 1–2 hours. Timing depends primarily on how expertly you handle the battery-powered, two-wheeled transport.

Mr. Sedona Private Guides (928/204-2201, http://mrsedona.com) lead half- and full-day tours geared to your abilities and interests, from gentle strolls and vortex adventures to down-right challenging hikes. **Sedona Vortex Tours** (150 State Route 179, 928/282-2733, www.se-donaretreats.com) can customize a trip to visit a medicine wheel or include a Native American ceremony.

You can also opt for yoga hikes, botanical walks, shamanic journeys, or fly-fishing expeditions—if you need help making a selection, stop in at the Chamber of Commerce Visitor Center (1 Forest Rd., 928/282-7722 or 800/288-7336, www.visitsedona.com, 8:30 A.M.–5 P.M. Mon.–Sat., 8 A.M.–3 P.M. Sun.), or ask local hotels or stores for recommendations.

Air Tours

Arizona Helicopter Adventures (235 Air Terminal Dr., 928/282-0904, www.azheli.com) skims massive buttes and green forests on routes like the Red Rock Roundup ($65 per person), which surveys the area's best-known formations, incuding Bell and Snoopy Rocks, as well as the Chapel of the Holy Cross.

Take to the skies in a helicopter or Red Waco biplane with **Sedona Air Tours** (1225 Airport Rd., 928/204-5939, www.sedonaairtours.com). Biplane flights can accommodate two passengers at a time, while a pilot provides commentary about the landscape. Tours range from the 20-minute Classic Tour ($99 per person)—which soars past Bell Rock, the Chapel of the Holy Cross, and other landmarks—to an hour-long flight through Sedona and Oak Creek ($489 per person). Combination trips that incorporate Jeep tours, fishing, white-water rafting, and flights to the Grand Canyon and Monument Valley are available.

THE VORTEX BUZZ

© KATHLEEN BRYANT

Cathedral Rock's spires are said to be an energy vortex.

Sedona's vortexes embody much of the city's New Age culture: an ever-present phenomenon

that earns curiosity from locals and visitors alike. You may be familiar with more mundane vortexes, like the desert's spiraling dust devils or water going down a drain. Sedona's vortexes are centers of energy—invisible and immeasurable by practical means—that believers say lead to heightened self-awareness and spiritual experiences.

Depending on whom you ask, numerous sites are scattered around town, but there are four well-known and easy-to-reach vortexes: the saddle of Airport Mesa, Boynton Canyon, Bell Rock, and Cathedral Rock. Some are associated with masculine energy, improving strength and self-confidence, while others are more feminine, boosting patience and kindness. But don't take anyone's word for it: See for yourself where your inner journey leads.

If you're a nonbeliever, you might try thinking of vortexes as beautiful natural spots that offer an opportunity for reflection. You could also view them as an introduction to Sedona's metaphysical side, because if you've ever wanted to experience a psychic reading or explore alternative healing techniques, you're in the right place. The local chamber of commerce even has an affinity group for member businesses that focus on the metaphysical (www.sedonaspiritual.com).

Astronomy Tour

Sedona's clean air, low humidity, and dark skies provide the perfect backdrop for shimmering planets, galaxies, and thousands upon thousands of stars. **Sedona Stargazing Tours** (928/853-9778, www.eveningskytours.com, $60 adults, $35 ages 6–12) survey the nighttime canopy with custom-built telescopes that offer so-close-you-can-touch-it views of the moon, meteor showers, and even Saturn's rings. Professional astronomers act as guides, beginning with an overview of the night's celestial display before turning telescopes over to guests.

BALLOONING

Though several ballooning companies advertise tours, only two are permitted by the Coconino National Forest to fly in the red-rock area, so be sure to verify routes when booking with other companies. Tours begin at sunrise, when the air is still and sunlight reaches across the landscape. Your reward for the early start is seeing the red rocks emerge from purple shadows to be burnished in gold.

Northern Light Balloon Expeditions (800/230-6222 or 928/282-2274, www.northernlightballoon.com, $195 per person) has been floating over the red rocks since 1974. Their balloons carry no more than seven passengers, for a personalized feel. (Groups of up to 35 are accommodated in separate balloons.) Flights, approximately an hour long, are followed by a champagne picnic and include transportation to your hotel. Day-before reservations are usually available.

Red Rock Balloon Adventures (800/258-3754, www.redrockballoons.com, $195 person) also offers 60- to 90-minute sunrise tours, concluding with a mimosa picnic. Brides and grooms may want to consider the Wedding Package ($2,500), which can accommodate up to six people on a private flight and includes a "commemorative picnic" with wedding cake.

HIKING

Hikers, welcome to a paradise of spectacular scenery, massive geological formations, and acres upon acres of protected land. It's easy to use a succession of clichés to describe the views from Sedona's trails (breathtaking, heart-stopping, etc.), but it's hard to convey the riches of experiences you'll find when you enter the landscape on foot. Even if you're not a hiker, you can't help but enjoy a stroll among red-rock monuments or along the lush banks of Oak Creek. With more than 200 miles of trails to choose from, you're sure to find one that matches your skill level and schedule. For maps and advice, stop by an official visitor center or contact the forest service's Red Rock Ranger District (8375 State Route 179, 928/203-7500, www.redrockcountry.org, 8 A.M.–5 P.M. daily).

The **Courthouse Loop** (four-mile loop) is a fine introductory trail. Beginning on the Bell Rock Pathway just north of the Village of Oak Creek on State Route 179. The trail is often busy, and for good reason: it's beautiful. The leisurely route circles Bell Rock (considered a vortex) and Courthouse Butte, making it a can't-miss trek for families and first-time hikers.

About a mile north on State Route 179, turn onto Back O' Beyond Road and proceed to the parking lot for the **Cathedral Rock Trail** (1.5 miles round-trip). The short but steep hike to the heart of Cathedral Rock (another vortex) is challenging, especially for acrophobes, but the views from the formation's central spires are a big reward. Follow the cairns (rock markers), and be prepared to use toeholds carved into the rock to ascend a particularly steep section.

In West Sedona, the **Airport Mesa Trail** (4.5-mile loop) provides a series of camera-ready vistas of Sedona and its red-rock buttes. It's best to hit this trail early in the morning before the parking lot—about halfway up Airport Road—fills up.

From State Route 89A, turn north on

Soldiers Pass Road and follow the brown signs marking a small parking area for the **Soldier Pass Trail** (four miles round-trip). Highlights include Devil's Kitchen (a large sinkhole) and Seven Sacred Pools, a series of natural basins eroded into the bedrock of Soldier Wash. Just after the trail crosses the boundary of the Red Rock–Secret Mountain Wilderness, a challenging quarter-mile spur heads right, up to a series of arches.

The **Devil's Bridge Trail** (two miles round-trip) leads to the area's largest natural stone arch. To get to the trailhead from West Sedona, take Dry Creek Road north to Forest Road 152, where you'll need a four-wheel-drive vehicle to continue another 1.5 miles to the parking area. At about three-quarters of a mile into the moderate hike, the trail splits, the right fork going to the end of the arch, the left winding below it. Be prepared to climb stone-slab stairs, which do not have handrails, and do heed the forest service's warning not to stand atop the arch. (Geology happens, sometimes over eons, sometimes suddenly.)

Park just outside Enchantment Resort to trek the **Boynton Canyon Trail** (five miles round-trip) an easy to moderate hike that traverses several different terrains, from cactus-dotted desert to pine-shaded forest. As you make your way up the canyon, pause to look up at shady alcoves in the cliffs: Many shelter prehistoric Sinagua dwellings. The cocooning box canyon is said to be imbued with vortex energy, and for the Yavapai people, it is an important location in tribal history. The canyon's entrance is guarded by the tall, elegant spire referred to as **Kachina Woman,** accessible from the intersecting Vista Trail (0.5 mile round-trip).

Just west of the resort on Boynton Pass Road, a large paved parking area marks the start of the **Fay Canyon Trail** (2.5 miles round-trip). Scrub oak and ponderosa pines shade much of this relatively level trail. Less than a mile into the trek, look for an easy-to-miss side trail,

The Fay Canyon Trail's sandstone cliffs are streaked with mineral deposits.

which leads to a natural stone arch. A bit farther down the main trail, look midway up the canyon walls for a red sandstone spire that resembles a goblet or mace.

BIKING

Mountain bikers will find some of the best off-roading in the country, across a terrain every bit as diverse and challenging as meccas in Moab, Utah, and Durango, Colorado—though far less crowded. The single-track trails lure diehards and beginners alike, thanks to challenging combinations of dirt, sand, and slickrock.

Many of Sedona's hiking trails accommodate bikers, the most notable exceptions being designated wilderness trails where bikes are strictly forbidden. Consult maps or trailhead signage before setting out or, better yet, stop by one of the local bike shops for friendly advice. Always exercise caution on rock formations and near cliff edges.

© KATHLEEN BRYANT

Teapot Rock near Schnebly Hill

The **Jim Thompson Trail** (five miles round-trip) can be accessed from the end of Jordan Road in Uptown Sedona or a couple of miles north at the Wilson Canyon Trailhead at the Midgley Bridge on State Route 89A. Thompson built this rocky trail in the 1880s as a wagon road to his cabin. The wide route passes beneath the "sail" of Ship Rock and neighboring Steamboat Rock, offering views of Uptown and the colorful Schnebly Hill rock formations.

For a moderately challenging half-day trek, try the **Submarine Loop** (10 miles), beginning on the Broken Arrow hiking trail at the end of Morgan Road, which lies east of State Route 179 south of Sedona. The trail changes from dirt single-track to slickrock at Submarine Rock and Chicken Point. Make this a loop by circling around the west side of Twin Buttes on the Little Horse trail to the Bell Rock Pathway, then using neighborhood streets to pick up the Mystic trail and return to Morgan Road.

Starting at the high school west of Sedona,

the **Red Rock Pathways Multi-Use Trail** gives bikers a safer alternative to State Route 89A for accessing a network of trails and forest roads along **Lower Red Rock Loop Road.** Options include traveling through **Red Rock State Park** and crossing Oak Creek to the Turkey Creek Road, which intersects with Verde Valley School Road. From here, you can return to the loop road via Red Rock Crossing. Or you might take the challenging trail across Scheurman Mountain, which connects the Upper and Lower Red Rock Loops.

If you need to rent some wheels, **Sedona Bike & Bean** (6020 State Route 179, 928/284-0210, www.bike-bean.com, 8 A.M.–5 P.M. daily) in the Village of Oak Creek offers convenient access to trails near Bell, Courthouse, and Cathedral Rocks. The laid-back shop rents mountain and road bikes starting at $25 for two hours, and same-day reservations are welcome on any bike for any length of time. The coffee's pretty darn good, too. Inquire about the Bean's tours, which include family-friendly mountain biking and road tours to wineries and galleries. A new location near Uptown (671 State Route 179, 928/204-5666, 8 A.M.–5 P.M. daily) specializes in road bikes.

Over the Edge Sports (1695 W. State Route 89A, 928/282-1106, http://otesports. com, 9 A.M.–6 P.M. daily) caters to the fat-tire crowd, though they also rent spiffy Italian road bikes. Prices start at $30 per day and rise to $80 for premium-suspension bikes. You'll find maps and trail advice here, along with custom Sedona jerseys and other gear. They host group rides; stop in and chat with the friendly staff to find out what's on the calendar.

BIRDING

More than 300 bird species flock to the Verde Valley's lush riparian areas, woodlands, and forests, making the region a prime spot for bird-watching. Throughout the year, it's not uncommon to see ravens, eagles, great blue herons, orioles, canyon wrens, and several species of hawks. Canada geese, kingfishers, mergansers, ducks, and other waterfowl winter in Oak Creek Canyon and the wetlands created by the treatment ponds west of Sedona. A good place to see black hawks (a threatened species) is along the creek in **Red Rock State Park** (4050 Red Rock Loop Rd., 928/282-6907, http://azstateparks.com/parks/rero, 8 A.M.–5 P.M. daily, $6 per vehicle), where volunteers lead daily bird walks.

Serious birders should consider timing a visit with the **Verde Valley Birding and Nature Festival** (www.birdyverde.org) held each April, featuring field trips led by local experts. An excellent guide, *Birding in Sedona and the Verde Valley,* is available from the Northern Arizona chapter of the **Audobon Society** (www.northernarizonaaudobon.org). If you forgot your binoculars, stop by **Jay's Bird Barn** (2370 W. State Route 89A, 928/203-5700, www.jaysbirdbarn.com, 8:30 A.M.–5:30 P.M. Mon.–Sat.) in the Safeway shopping center. They host bird walks on Wednesday mornings.

GOLF

For those who appreciate the pleasure of a golf course's design as much as the thrill of a challenging game, Sedona won't disappoint. Lush fairways provide a brilliant contrast to the crimson buttes that surround the area's courses. Sedona is "land-locked" by Coconino National Forest, keeping real estate at a premium: Thus, you can expect slightly shorter drives and imaginatively designed tees and greens.

If the scenery looks familiar at the **Sedona Golf Resort** (35 Ridge Trail Dr., 877/733-6630 or 928/284-2093, www.sedonagolfresort.com), you may recognize it from one of the classic westerns that were filmed here long before the carefully manicured greens and sandy bunkers arrived. The championship course in the Village of Oak Creek features long, rolling fairways and scenic vistas—including the view of Cathedral Rock from the signature tenth hole. *Golf Digest* regularly bestows the 6,646-yard, par-71 course with a well-deserved four-star rating. The clubhouse offers clinics, private and group lessons, and even a club-fitting analysis.

Purists who prefer a traditional layout will appreciate the **Oak Creek Country Club** (690 Bell Rock Blvd., 888/284-1660 or 928/284-1660, www.oakcreekcountryclub.com), also in the VOC. Robert Trent Jones Sr. and Robert Trent Jones Jr. designed the par-72, 18-hole championship golf course to be a tough play, with tree-lined fairways that dogleg, slightly elevated greens, and lakes that pose the occasional hazard. The signature fourth hole, which is complemented by terrific views of the red rocks, will push most golfers to earn a par 3.

Northwest of Sedona, incongruously tucked among wilderness canyons, **Seven Canyons** (755 Golf Club Way, 928/203-3001, www.sevencanyons.com) has earned accolades from golfers, including being named one of the Top

100 Modern Courses by *Golfweek* magazine. Tom Weiskopf designed the par-70 course to emphasize the natural topography of the landscape, with tees that take advantage of changes in elevation, naturally rolling fairways, and small, quick greens. Rock walls, water features, bridges, and high-desert landscaping are backdropped by red sandstone buttes and Maroon Mountain.

The par-3 executive course at the **Poco Diablo Resort** (1752 S. State Route 179, 928/282-7333, www.pocodiablo.com) provides an excellent opportunity to work on your short game while taking in some impressive views along Oak Creek. The duck ponds, willow and pine trees, and low-key atmosphere offer a refreshing break from Uptown's crowds. The water hazards and fast greens can be challenging, but the real draw to this nine-hole course is its manageable size, offering a quick and affordable way to fit in a game of golf on a short trip to Sedona.

SPAS

One of the finest spas in the world, **Mii Amo** (525 Boynton Canyon Rd., 888/749-2137, www.miiamo.com, 6 A.M.–10 P.M. daily) regularly tops "best of" lists for its comprehensive treatments, sleek decor, and incredible setting in Boynton Canyon. The luxury spa is only open to guests of Mii Amo or its sister resort, Enchantment, so consider splurging on a stay here—you won't be disappointed. You'll want to spend days relaxing by indoor and outdoor pools, enjoying a yoga class on the lawn, or taking a moment for quiet contemplation in the Crystal Grotto, which perfectly aligns with the sun's light during the summer solstice. Day packages for Enchantment guests start at $415, and prices for an all-inclusive three-night journey begin at $2,400.

Hilton Sedona Spa (10 Ridge View Dr., 928/284-6900, www.hiltonsedonaspa.com, 5:30 A.M.–8 P.M. Mon.–Fri., 7 A.M.–8 P.M.

Sat.–Sun.) boasts a devoted local membership who frequent the 25,000-square-foot facility for its gym, three tennis courts, outdoor heated lap pool, and fitness classes that range from basic cardio to tai chi, yoga, zumba, and qi gong. Hour-long massages, scrubs, and other treatments start at $140, and you can make a day of it by taking advantage of the separate men's and women's steam rooms, saunas, and rooftop sundecks.

The chic boutique **Spa at Sedona Rouge** (2250 W. State Route 89A, 928/340-5331, www.sedonarouge.com/spa, 10 A.M.–7 P.M. daily) offers substance along with style, as therapists are trained in a host of techniques, including ayurvedic treatments, Thai massage, Lomi Lomi, cranial sacral therapy, reflexology, and cupping massage. In addition to gender-specific steam rooms and alfresco whirlpools, guests can enjoy the coed tranquility room and garden. Massages here start at $120.

Amara Spa (100 Amara Ln., 800/891-0105 or 928/282-6088, www.amararesort.com, 10 A.M.–7 P.M. daily) is another mod boutique-resort option, with a decidedly luxe atmosphere. Guests can create a custom-tailored massage (starting at $120) or select from a menu of full-body treatments, like the Chakra-Balancing Scrub and Wrap ($180). Daily yoga classes and private fitness sessions are available.

Sedona Spa (160 Portal Ln., 928/282-5108, www.sedonaspa.com, 6 A.M.–9 P.M. Mon.–Sat., 8 A.M.–6 P.M. Sun.) at Los Abrigados Resort offers an impressive selection of therapeutic massages that begin at $95, as well as acupuncture and full-body polishes, herbal wraps, and soothing mud masks. Get to the spa early to relax in the eucalyptus steam room, sauna, and whirlpool, or to fit in a game of tennis or a Pilates class.

Therapy on the Rocks (676 N. State Route 89 A, 928/282-3002, www.therapyontherocks. org, 9 A.M.–5:30 P.M. Mon.–Sat.), housed in a cottage just north of Uptown on Oak Creek, specializes in myofascial release, a massage technique practitioners say relieves pain and increases range of motion. There are half-hour, hour, and half-day sessions, as well as comprehensive two-week programs for people with chronic pain conditions. If it's warm enough, you can enjoy a creekside treatment or the outdoor whirlpool on the sundeck. Customized treatments vary from person to person; call ahead for prices.

In West Sedona, **New Day Spa** (1449 W. State Route 89A, 928/282-7502, www.sedonanewdayspa.com, 9 A.M.–7 P.M. Mon.–Sat., 10 A.M.–7 P.M. Sun.) may not have resort surroundings, but it offers a full menu of massages and treatments that start at $115. Many of the spa products are formulated in Sedona from essential oils and native herbs.

Sedona is known for its alternative therapies,
and even at larger resorts the lines between spa treatments and healing modalities tend to blur. Skilled local practitioners of acupuncture, reflexology, ayurveda, hypnotherapy, or other integrative modalities might work in a hotel spa, a small studio, or both. In the Village of Oak Creek, **Ayurveda Sedona** (70 Navajo Rd., 928/284-1114, http://ayurvedasedona.com) adds treatments like shirodhara or marma point therapy to massage. At **Lovejoy's Enchanted Cottage** (235 Birch Blvd., 928/301-1903, deblovejoy.com) in West Sedona, a pampering pedicure can be combined with reflexology, aromatherapy, reiki, and other energy work. West Sedona's **Thunder Mountain Wellness** (2940 Southwest Dr., 928/202-2273, www.tmwc.org) offers yoga therapy and somatic bodywork in addition to massage.

Accommodations

More than a century ago, T. C. and Sedona Schnebly rented rooms to guests in their wood-frame house along Oak Creek, where Tlaquepaque now stands. Sedona's tradition of hospitality continues today. Though a few chain hotels have popped up among the mom-and-pop motels and luxury resorts, the town's specialty is the romantic getaway—charming inns, B&Bs, and lodges. Rates peak in the fall and spring, though you'll be able to find discounts if you stay midweek, or visit during summer or winter months. Lively and walkable Uptown has a village feel, while West Sedona offers the convenience of nearby service businesses. A few miles south, the Village of Oak Creek has budget options (and half the sales tax), with some motels mere blocks from golf courses. No matter where you stay, everything is within a few minutes' drive, and even if your room doesn't have a view, red-rock panoramas are never very far away.

UPTOWN AND HIGHWAY 179
$50-100
Star Motel (295 Jordan Rd., 928/282-3641, starmotelsedona.com, $80–90 d) is an ideal spot for budget travelers looking for affordability with a little character. The motel was built in the 1950s, and its 11 units are bright and clean. The hospitable owners, Marcelle and Anne, couldn't be sweeter. Families will love the second-floor suite's two queen beds, full kitchen, and private patio with views of the red rocks.

The Sedona Motel (218 State Route 179, 928/282-7187, www.thesedonamotel.com, $90–110 d) is a good value. The motel's terraced patio has commanding views of the red rocks, and the central location just south of the 89A/179 intersection is within walking distance of Tlaquepaque or Uptown.

© KATHLEEN BRYANT

It's easy to find a room with a view in Uptown Sedona.

$100-250

Along the banks of Oak Creek below Uptown's shops and galleries, **Amara Hotel, Restaurant & Spa** (100 Amara Ln., 928/282-4828, www.amararesort.com, $185–215 d) brings a bit of big-city chic to Red Rock Country. The posh boutique hotel stands out among Sedona's ubiquitous Southwestern style, though its minimalist design doesn't try to overshadow its natural setting among giant sycamore trees and spectacular views. You'll find all the usual luxury amenities—300-thread-count linens, oversize soaking tubs, private balconies, elegantly manicured grounds—but Amara ups the game with a heated saltwater pool and the Hundred Rox restaurant.

You can't beat the location of **◖ The Orchards Inn** (254 N. State Route 89A, 800/474-7719 or 928/282-2405, www.orchardsinn.com, $200–240 d). A block from Uptown's main drag, the inn's contemporary

Southwestern rooms have patios and decks with views of Snoopy Rock and the surrounding buttes. If a "room with a view" is a priority, this may be an ideal place to hang your hat, and the recently renovated hotel includes welcome amenities for the price. Uptown's shops, restaurants, and bars are just outside your front door, and the on-site **Taos Cantina** serves lunch and dinner.

The **Matterhorn Inn** (230 Apple Ave., 800/372-8207 or 928/282-7176, www.matterhorninn.com, $160–180 d) is only steps from Uptown Sedona's shops, galleries, and restaurants. Thanks to its hillside location, each of the hotel's 23 rooms has a private balcony or terrace with panoramic views of Snoopy Rock, Camel's Head, and Teapot Rock. The hotel has a hot tub and a seasonal pool, making it a favorite choice for families.

Next to the Sedona Arts Center, **Best Western Arroyo Roble Hotel & Creekside Villas** (400 N. State Route 89A, 800/773-3662 or 928/282-4001, www.bestwesternsedona.com, $225–265 d) has a host of amenities you typically would find at a large resort: tennis and racquetball courts, a fully equipped exercise room, and an indoor/outdoor heated swimming pool. Some rooms in the five-story hotel even have fireplaces and whirlpool tubs, and roomy two-bedroom villas along the creek are just steps away from shady paths.

Los Abrigados Resort & Spa (160 Portal Ln., 928/282-1777, www.ilxresorts.com, $180–280 d), operated by Diamond Resorts, sits on a historical property at the heart of Sedona, where T. C. and Sedona Schnebly built a two-story frame home in the early 1900s. Walking the 22-acre, beautifully landscaped resort next to Tlaquepaque and Oak Creek, you'll find plenty of diversions: two swimming pools, a whirlpool spa, tennis and basketball courts, a fitness center, and a creekside miniature golf course. Plus, the on-site Sedona Spa features some fine treatments for guests looking for a little R&R.

A classic B&B, the **Creekside Inn at Sedona** (99 Copper Cliffs Dr., 800/390-8621 or 928/282-4992, www.creeksideinn.net, $200–270 d) is decorated with period antiques, and its six cheerful rooms and suites are bright and clean. The Creekview Suite has a mammoth, ceiling-high walnut bed and French doors leading to a private deck, ideal for a romantic getaway. Guests can pass the time by fishing in the creek on the three-acre property, relaxing on the porch with a glass of wine, or taking a short stroll along Gallery Row.

On the site of a former CCC camp and movie soundstage, the **Kings Ransom Motel** (771 State Route 179, 800/846-6164 or 928/282-7151, www.kingsransomsedona.com, $80–150 d) and neighboring **Kings Ransom Inn** (725 State Route 179, 877/480-0044 or 928/282-3132, http://kingsransominn.com, $115–180 d) sit at the end of Gallery Row, a short walk from shops and forest service trails. Rooms at the motel have balconies or patio access, some with views of the lovely courtyard pool or the red rocks. Views are also included with the free continental breakfast, which you can enjoy in the dining room or on the courtyard deck.

About halfway between Uptown and the Village of Oak Creek, **Radisson Poco Diablo Resort** (1752 State Route 179, 877/282-5755 or 928/282-7333, www.pocodiablo.com, $200–240 d) offers a peaceful, creekside setting with red-rock views and nearby hiking, as well as the amenities of a larger resort, including a fitness center, a swimming pool, a nine-hole golf course, and tennis courts. Select rooms have a fireplace and private whirlpool bath. The on-site restaurant, **T. Carl's,** serves breakfast, lunch, and dinner.

Over $250

☾ L'Auberge de Sedona (301 L'Auberge Ln.,

855/905-5745, www.lauberge.com, $400–650 d) seduces guests with its warm, friendly atmosphere, thoughtful service, and romantic setting along the banks of Oak Creek. The intimate resort feels hidden away under giant sycamores, and the morning duck feedings and relaxing spa feel a world away from the congestion and crowds just up the hill in Uptown. Cozy rooms are available in the main lodge, though the creekside cabins are worth the splurge. The new hillside cottages are refreshingly modern, boasting outdoor showers and large observation decks. Be sure to savor at least one meal at the property's award-winning restaurant along the creek.

One of Arizona's finest hotels, **☾ El Portal Sedona** (95 Portal Ln., 800/313-0017 or 928/203-9405, www.elportalsedona.com, $260–400 d) blends Arts-and-Crafts design with Southwestern touches and hacienda-style hospitality. Owners Connie and Steve Segner have created a luxurious, intimate inn with a commitment to even the smallest details. Each of the 12 unique rooms and suites echoes El Portal's eclectic historical style—stained-glass doors, cozy fireplaces, antique furnishings, thick adobe walls, and private gardens. Situated next to Tlaquepaque, the inn is only a short stroll from some of Sedona's best restaurants and galleries, but you may not want to leave this elegant hideaway. (If you're on a budget, don't despair: Midweek rates, last-minute deals, and summer specials can make this dream stay a reality.)

WEST SEDONA
$50-100

Cheap, clean, and convenient, **Sugar Loaf Lodge** (1870 W. State Route 89A, 928/282-9451, www.sedonasugarloaf.com, $60–90 d) provides the basics just off of State Route 89A and even throws in a few frills like a pool, free wireless Internet, and in-room refrigerators. The motel isn't fancy, but its low price is hard to beat, as is the convenient access to neighboring hiking and mountain biking trails.

Recently refurbished, the **Baby Quail Inn** (50 Willow Way, 866/977-8245 or 928/282-2835, $85–95) has clean rooms and welcome amenities like free wireless Internet, in-room refrigerators and microwaves, and a complimentary breakfast. The tidy little property makes the most of its space with a quiet patio and outdoor hot tub, tucked into in a residential neighborhood just off State Route 89A.

$100-250

Sky Ranch Lodge (1105 Airport Rd., 888/708-6400 or 928/282-6400, www.skyranchlodge.com, $105–180 d) is a pleasant throwback to a 1970s ranch or vacation home. Rooms are plain-Jane, but chances are you'll spend most of your time enjoying the property and its views, especially if you've requested a private deck or rim-view cottage. Small ponds, bridges, and grassy lawns dot the six-acre property, with quaint stone paths leading to quiet gardens and a secluded swimming pool. Best of all, the inn is perched on Airport Mesa, 500 feet above Sedona, providing elevated views of the town and its red-rock formations. When you're ready to venture from this mesa-top haven, a five-minute drive will drop you back in the heart of West Sedona.

Perched on a hillside, the **Best Western Inn of Sedona** (1200 W. State Route 89A, 800/292-6344 or 928/282-3072, www.innofsedona.com, $150–180 d) has a sensitive, slope-hugging design with four terraced balconies that boast 360-degree views of the red rocks. The rooms are clean and comfortable—with surprising touches like glass-bowl sinks in the bathroom—and the hotel throws in a long list of amenities, including an outdoor pool, a breakfast buffet, an in-town shuttle, free wireless Internet, and concierge services, as well as a free shuttle to/from Uptown.

The Lodge at Sedona (125 Kallof Pl.,

800/619-4467 or 928/204-1942, www.lodgeatsedona.com, $210–300 d) is a surprisingly secluded retreat in the midst of West Sedona. The lodge is decorated in gracious Mission style, with cozy, fireside seating areas and a handsome dining room that serves as a gathering spot for gourmet breakfasts and sunset treats. Second-story guest rooms offer red-rock views, and king suites on the main level have private decks. The lodge's soothing gardens incorporate water features and a labyrinth for meditative walks.

The Santa Fe–style **Southwest Inn at Sedona** (3250 W. State Route 89A, 800/483-7422 or 928/282-3344, www.swinn.com, $140–170 d) is a comfortable place to sleep, with excellent bedding, gas fireplaces, roomy baths, and other resort-worthy amenities in a welcoming B&B atmosphere. It's located near Dry Creek Road, with convenient access to the library and trailheads. Be sure to ask for a room with a view.

Sedona Rouge Hotel & Spa (2250 W. State Route 89A, 866/312-4111 or 928/203-4111, www.sedonarouge.com, $240–310 d) combines clean, contemporary lines with Mediterranean flair, accented in deep reds. The comfortable, well-appointed rooms on the second and third levels feature generous walk-in showers with dual heads. This hotel has a more urban vibe than some of its competitors, while still honoring the natural setting, particularly from the Observation Terrace, open at night for stargazing. Plus, you'll find other amenities, like a large outdoor seating area with fireplace, a heated swimming pool and Jacuzzi, a top-notch spa, and the on-site restaurant **Reds**.

The name **Boots and Saddles** (2900 Hopi Dr., 800/201-1944 or 928/282-1944, www.oldwestbb.com, $250–295 d) suggests plenty of Western style, and you'll get it at this popular bed-and-breakfast. Innkeepers Irith and Sam Raz have earned a loyal following, thanks to their warm hospitality and sumptuous breakfasts. Each of the inn's six rooms is theme-decorated, with amenities that vary from fireplaces and outdoor air-jet tubs to telescopes for stargazing. The 600-square-foot City Slickers suite boasts lots of rich leather and a sunny breakfast nook.

The **Alma De Sedona Inn** (50 Hozoni Dr., 800/923-2282 or 928/282-2737, www.almadesedona.com, $190–260 d) is a lovely bed-and-breakfast for those who appreciate a little privacy with their red-rock views. The 12 large rooms have king-size beds, gas fireplaces, and two-person tubs. The grounds are well maintained and feature a host of desert cacti and agave, along with shady sycamores. Plenty of poolside seating means you can breakfast alfresco.

Somewhat ordinary on the outside, **Sedona Real Inn & Suites** (95 Arroyo Piñon Dr., 800/353-1239 or 928/282-1414, www.sedonareal.com, $155–235 d) has clean, comfortable, spacious rooms and suites, making it a good option for families and groups. This family-owned hotel offers perks not found at budget competitors: free high-speed Internet, an outdoor pool and spa, complimentary breakfast, room service, private balconies, and outstanding concierge service.

Cathedral Rock Lodge & Retreat Center (61 W. Los Amigos Lane, 928/282-5560, www.cathedralrocklodge.com, $150–300) isn't fancy, but its views of Cathedral Rock are unmatched. Situated near Red Rock Crossing, about 15 minutes from Uptown, the lodge's three secluded cabins are surrounded by green lawns and wooded grounds. The largest, Homestead House, sleeps up to six people, offering a roomy kitchen, two bedrooms, two bathrooms, and a collection of westerns filmed in Sedona ready to pop into the DVD player.

Over $250

You won't find a hotel in Sedona with a more stunning backdrop than **Enchantment Resort** (525 Boynton Canyon Rd., 800/826-4180 or 928/282-2900, www.enchantmentresort.com, $425–825 d). Situated 10 minutes outside of town, the resort's 70 acres are nestled within the soaring cliffs of Boynton Canyon, creating a sense of seclusion and protection. A recent $25 million makeover gave the resort and its casitas a sophisticated yet earthy flair. Guests have exclusive access to swimming pools, tennis courts, lawn games, pitch-and-putt golf, resort trails, and the adjacent Mii Amo spa, one of the finest in the world. Kids will enjoy spending time at Camp Coyote, with its focus on Native American culture and the Southwestern environment.

◖ **Mii Amo** (525 Boynton Canyon Rd., 928/282-2900, www.miiamo.com) sets the bar for spa retreats, blending holistic treatments, Native American traditions, and luxury pampering. Mii Amo's seamless indoor/outdoor design blends chic, modern style with Boynton Canyon's soaring red cliffs, a soothing yet stimulating backdrop for three-, four- and seven-night "personal journeys" tailored to each guest's goals: de-stress, spiritual exploration, etc. Rates begin at $1,600/night for a three-night package, which includes accommodations in one of 16 spa casitas and suites, three meals a day, and two spa treatments every day, as well as fitness classes, spa amenities, and activities like tennis, hiking, and mountain biking. The small, communal setting is perfect for solo travelers who want to balance personal time and socializing.

Subtle isn't the word for **Adobe Grand Villas** (35 Hozoni Dr., 800/900-7616 or 928/203-7616, www.adobegrandvillas.com, $399–699 d), where themed "mansion-style" suites start at 850 square feet, each with at least one king-size bed and two fireplaces. (One suite has lantern chandeliers and a canopy bed designed to look like a Conestoga wagon.) Some rooms feature steam showers and tubs for two, while others offer red-rock views, private patios, and wood-beam ceilings.

VILLAGE OF OAK CREEK
$50-150

Tucked into a corner of Bell Rock Plaza, **Sedona Village Lodge** (105 Bell Rock Plaza, 800/890-0521 or 928/284-3626, www.sedonalodge.com, $50–90) offers basic accommodation at budget prices. The standard rooms include wireless Internet, and for another $30, the suites have microwaves, refrigerators, and gas fireplaces.

Wildflower Inn (6086 State Route 179, 928/284-3937, www.sedonawildflowerinn.com, $99–210 d) is nicer than your standard chain motel fare, with superb views of Bell Rock from some rooms. Expect a few pleasant perks like flat-screen TVs, an in-room fridge, and continental breakfast. Be sure to call the motel directly for any late-breaking deals.

$150-300

Bordering the national forest, ◀ **Adobe Village Graham Inn** (150 Canyon Circle Dr., 800/228-1425 or 928/284-1425, www.adobevillagegrahaminn.com, $180–360 d) promises a bit of "rustic luxury" and doesn't disappoint. The boutique inn's unique rooms and villas have an earthy but romantic ambience. The Sundance offers a fireplace, wood-plank flooring, king-size canopy bed, and large bathroom with a rainforest shower and jet tub. The Wilderness Villa has peeled pine walls, a charming periwinkle-blue sleigh bed, and a river-rock fireplace that connects the bedroom with a two-person tub. The small gardens and incomparable views of Bell, Cathedral, and Courthouse Rocks make this bed-and-breakfast a real gem.

Adobe Hacienda Bed & Breakfast (10 Rojo Dr., 800/454-7191, www.adobe-hacienda.com, $210–300 d) has four guest rooms and a casita, each decorated with traditional Southwestern touches, like lodgepole beams, Saltillo tile floors, Native American rugs, hand-painted Mexican sinks, and cozy Pendleton blankets. Owners Pauline and Brad Staub are consummate hosts, happy to point you in the direction of an easy hiking trail or to serve up a hearty breakfast on the flagstone patio that overlooks the adjacent golf course and the red rocks. Call for last-minute discounts or to request a specific room.

Families will appreciate the **Hilton Sedona Resort & Spa** (90 Ridge Trail Dr., 928/284-4040, www.hiltonsedona.com, $260–310 d), which provides an impressively diverse assortment of amenities, including a championship golf course, a fitness center, a full-service spa, and multiple pools. Guest rooms and one-bedroom suites—which can accommodate up to five—are tastefully decorated and boast gas fireplaces and small balconies overlooking the fairways or red rocks. Perched on a ridge above the Village of Oak Creek, the hotel's location far from the crowds of Uptown can provide a nice change of pace.

If you are planning to spend more than a few days in Sedona, **Las Posadas of Sedona** (26 Avenida De Piedras, 928/284-5288, www.lasposadasofsedona.com, $180–220 d) will make you feel at home with roomy, amenity-rich suites featuring private entrances, desks, double-sided fireplaces, and kitchenettes. The boutique inn's French-trained chef goes above and beyond every morning to create a three-course Southwestern-style breakfast.

Food

As in many tourist towns, Sedona's dining options can be hit or miss—a divine meal one night, followed the next night by a so-so offering from the same restaurant. The inconsistency can be maddening, but your options are many: Mom-and-pop cafés, ethnic eateries, casual bistros, Western steakhouses, and elegant resort dining rooms. Many have picture-window views or charming patios, and a fair number are accommodating to vegetarians, who can dine well in Sedona. The food may be a bit pricier than you're used to, but go ahead and splurge at least once at one of the romantic dining spots that make a stay in Red Rock Country such a treat. If you're a night owl, be warned: Most Sedona restaurants stop serving before 9 p.m.

UPTOWN AND HIGHWAY 179
American

Dine inside the glam contemporary **Hundred Rox** (100 Amara Ln., 928/340-8859, www.amararesort.com/dining, 7 a.m.–9 p.m. daily, $20–30) in Uptown's Amara Resort or under the stars on the restaurant's patio. The innovative menu runs from updated American comfort food to global flavors, such as fresh spring rolls, duck schnitzel, and chicken piccata. Most weekends and a few weeknights, the lounge hosts local musicians.

One of the few spots in town where you can dine relatively late, **Sound Bites Grill** (101 N. State Route 89A, 928/282-2713, www.soundbitesgrille.com, 11 a.m.–11 p.m. Tues.–Sun., till midnight Fri.–Sat., $12–45), located in Piñon Pointe shops has a wide-ranging menu and live entertainment most nights.

Ken's Creekside (251 State Route 179, 928/282-1705, www.kenscreekside.com, 7:30 a.m.–10 p.m. daily, $14–33) has a pleasant and shady second-story patio and a varied menu that has a little bit of everything from seafood

and steak to creative vegetarian entrées. The lounge features infusion drinks, and on busy weekends, a late-night menu may be available.

Enjoy Sedona's award-winning microbrew at **Oak Creek Brewery & Grill** (336 State Route 179, 928/282-3300, www.oakcreekpub.com, 11:30 a.m.–8:30 p.m. daily, $12–26). The comfortable second-story pub at Tlaquepaque serves sandwiches, salads, pastas, burgers, and "fire-kissed" pizzas, like the feta-olive-and-artichoke Oak Creek Greek. Check out the refreshing ales and pilsners brewing in copper tanks behind the bar before heading out to the patio, where you'll have tree-house views of Snoopy Rock.

"Peak views" are also on the menu at **Shugrue's Hillside Grill** (671 State Route 179, 928/282-5300, http://shugrueshillside.com, 11:30 a.m.–3 p.m. and 5–8:30 p.m. daily, $14–36). Seafood—such as lemon-seared scallops or the signature flame-broiled shrimp scampi—is the house specialty, but in addition you'll find a wide selection of pastas, salads, and steaks, along with a few vegetarian options.

Asian

Thoughtful details like paper lanterns, handmade pottery, and rustic wooden furnishings give **🄲 Takashi** (465 Jordan Rd., 928/282-2334, www.takashisedona.com, 4–9 p.m. Tues.–Sun., plus lunch Tues. and Fri., $20–25) an air of traditional Japan. The tree-shaded patio is a peaceful oasis a block from Uptown's busy strip, and the classic menu includes sukiyaki, teppanyaki, sushi, teriyaki, and tempura. Save some room for the green tea ice cream.

Tucked behind the shops along Uptown's main drag, **Thai Palace** (260 Van Deren Rd., 928/282-8424, www.thaipalacesedona.com, 11 a.m.–9 p.m. Tues.–Sun., $13–16) has a delightful patio and a cozy but elegant dining room. The menu includes classic curry and noodle dishes, spiced to your preference.

Breakfast and Lunch

The sandwiches and salads at **Sedona Memories** (321 Jordan Rd., 928/282-0032, 10 A.M.–2 P.M. Mon.–Fri., $5–10) won't bust your budget (though you may have to loosen your belt a couple notches). This cash-only, mom-and-pop shop has a few tables outside, or you can head for one of Red Rock Country's plentiful picnic spots. Hint: Whether you plan to eat here or on the trail, if you call in your order ahead of time, you'll get a free cookie.

Located in the Hyatt Piñon Pointe shops, **Wildflower Bread Company** (101 N. State Route 89A, 928/204-2223, www.wildflowerbread.com, 6 A.M.–9 P.M. Mon.–Fri., 7 A.M.–9 P.M. Sat., 7 A.M.–8 P.M. Sun., $5–9) has pastries, soups, salads, pastas, and sandwiches made with fresh, hearty bread. (It's part of the ever-expanding Fox restaurant chain that has staked out many locations in Arizona.)

The **Secret Garden Café at Tlaquepaque** (336 State Route 179, 928/203-9564, www.sedonasecretgardencafe.com, 9 A.M.–5 P.M. daily, $7–13) is a pleasant place to enjoy breakfast, especially in the shady, flower-filled garden. Try the French toast dipped in Grand Marnier or a hearty breakfast burrito. In the afternoon, the café serves salads, sandwiches, burgers, and their signature deep-dish quiche.

A favorite with locals, **Señor Bob's** (841 State Route 179, 928/282-0131, www.senorbobshotdogs.com, 10:30 A.M.–5 P.M. daily, under $10) is a convenient place to grab a cup of coffee and a bratwurst or hot dog. (Yes, even a veggie dog.) Layer on the condiments and get back on the trail...or look for a seat on the small porch and watch the rest of the world drive past on their way to Uptown.

Desserts

If your taste buds are screaming for something sweet, you won't have to walk far to find relief in Uptown. A handful of confectionaries dot both sides of the highway, including the **Black Cow Café** (229 N. State Route 89A, 928/203-9868, daily, hours vary), an old-fashioned ice cream parlor where you can order a house-made waffle cone with a scoop or two of prickly pear, malted vanilla, espresso, and other flavors.

How Sweet It Is (336 State Route 179, 928/282-5455, 10 A.M.–6 P.M. daily) sells fudge, chocolates, lollipops, and an assortment of unique licorices, jelly beans, and other confections. This small sweetshop in Tlaquepaque also whips up fresh fruit smoothies, shakes, sundaes, and floats.

French

For a memorable setting, it's hard to top **L'Auberge Restaurant on Oak Creek** (301 L'Auberge Ln., 928/282-1661, www.lauberge.com, 7 A.M.–8 P.M. Mon.–Thurs., till 9 P.M. Fri.–Sat., $15–85). The restaurant's flagstone patio edges the banks of Oak Creek, and you can watch ducks glide past under a shady canopy of sycamores. A seasonal menu incorporates wild game and hearty soups in winter, shifting to fresh salads and creamy cheeses in summer. For dinner, three to five courses are available prix fixe. The champagne brunch, served Sundays 9 A.M.–2 P.M., is a special treat. Oenophiles will appreciate the wine menu, which has earned *Wine Spectator* magazine's "Award of Excellence" for more than 20 years.

A beloved Sedona landmark, **René at Tlaquepaque** (336 State Route 179, 928/282-9225, www.rene-sedona.com, 11:30 A.M.–2:30 P.M. and 5–8:30 P.M. daily, $15–45) draws locals and visitors celebrating weddings, anniversaries, and birthdays. The menu includes classics like French onion soup and roasted duck, as well as entrées with a Southwestern twist, like the antelope tenderloin with a whiskey-juniper berry sauce.

Italian

The Hideaway Restaurant (251 State Route 179, 928/282-4204, http://sedonahideawayrestaurant.com, 11 A.M.–9 P.M. daily, $7–20) is tucked into a small shopping center uphill from Tlaquepaque. This is where locals go for tasty subs, pastas, and pizzas, piled high with toppings like homemade sausage. You'll find plenty of kid-friendly choices—and a long deck above tree-lined Oak Creek, where you can enjoy views of Snoopy Rock and watch hummingbirds battling over feeders.

Mexican and Southwest

You might have to stand in line for the delicious and diverse Mexican cuisine at █ **Elote Café** (771 State Route 179, 928/203-0105, www.elotecafe.com, 5–9 P.M. Tues.–Sat., $17–25) because reservations aren't accepted at this popular spot. Chef Jeff Smedstad traveled through Mexico for more than 15 years, exploring regional flavors that he has combined for a menu of savory, slow-roasted meats and intriguing moles. Vegetarian selections are limited, but meat eaters will dine well on lamb adobo, braised buffalo ribs, smoked chicken enchiladas, and other flavorful creations.

The Mexican village atmosphere of Tlaquepaque provides a fitting backdrop for **El Rincon** (336 State Route 179, 928/282-4648, www.elrinconrestaurant.com, 11 A.M.–9 P.M. Tues.–Sat., 11 A.M.–8 P.M. Sun., 11 A.M.–4 P.M. Mon., $5–15), serving the classic Sonoran-style cuisine that most Americans recognize, including shredded-beef burritos, cheese enchiladas, and green corn tamales.

In the Hillside shops, **Javelina Cantina** (671 State Route 179, 928/282-1313, http://javelinacantinasedona.com, 11:30 A.M.–8:30 P.M. daily, $7–16) serves up the usual crowd-pleasers plus some fine fajitas—grilled beef, chicken, fish, or shrimp with sautéed onions, peppers, warm tortillas, guacamole, and crème fraîche. The large dining room and patio (with great views) are especially lively around dinnertime.

In Uptown, **Oaxaca Restaurant** (321 N. State Route 89A, 928/282-4179, http://oaxacarestaurant.com, 10 A.M.–9 P.M. daily, $12–20) offers stunning views of Sedona's red rocks, as well as great people-watching along the city's main drag. The menu includes familiar classics, plus lighter dishes and traditional ingredients like blue corn and nopales (cactus pads).

Steakhouses and Barbecue

If you have a hankering for cactus fries, buffalo burgers, or rattlesnake, settle into one of the big booths at **Cowboy Club Grille & Spirits** (241 N. State Route 89A, 928/282-4200, www.cowboyclub.com, 11 A.M.–10 P.M. daily, $10–37). Formerly the Oak Creek Tavern, where Joe Beeler and his artist friends founded the Cowboy Artists of America in 1965, this is now the place to go for cowboy-worthy steaks and ribs. You'll also find seafood, roast chicken or duck, barbecue, and even a few vegetarian options. Next door, the more upscale sibling, **Silver Saddle Room** (5–9 P.M. daily, $10–37), offers a similar menu in a more refined atmosphere.

Every town needs a hole-in-the-wall barbecue joint. Drop into **Sally's Mesquite BBQ & Grill** (250 Jordan Rd., 928/282-6533, www.sallysbbq.com, 11 A.M.–7 P.M. daily, $8–15) for a pulled pork sandwich, smoked beef brisket, or St. Louis–style ribs. The relaxed lunch and dinner spot has been serving up barbecue and classic sides like fresh-cut fries and homemade baked beans for more than 25 years.

At **Red Rock BBQ** (150 State Route 179, 928/204-5975, www.redrockbbq.com, 11 A.M.–9 P.M. Sun.–Thurs., 11 A.M.–10 P.M. Fri.–Sat., $9–15), you can dive into the hickory-smoked pork sandwiches, cornmeal-crusted catfish, and juicy hamburgers, or keep it light with one of the specialty salads. Sampler platters are great for sharing with family and friends, while you kick back on the patio and take in the views.

WINE NOT?

The **Verde Valley Wine Trail** (www.vvwine-trail.com) travels from the banks of Oak Creek in Page Springs to the mountainside town of Jerome. En route you'll discover an astonishing number of varietals, including charbono, Grenache, marsanne, merlot, mourvedre, petite sirah, pinot noir, sauvignon blanc, tempranillo, viognier, and zinfandel. Though the landscape is arid, many vineyards retain pioneering water rights granting them access to Oak Creek, the Verde River, or deep underground aquifers. Harvests run between late August and the end of September, but any time of year, you can stop by a tasting room to sample a flight for $5-10. Call a cab for transportation, or check out wine tours from **Sedona Adventure Tours** (877/673-3661, www.sedonaadventuretours.com).

PAGE SPRINGS ROAD

- **Javelina Leap Vineyards**
  (1565 Page Springs Rd., 928/649-2681, www.javelinaleapwinery.com, 11 A.M.-5 P.M. daily, cellar tours 11 A.M.-3 P.M. Fri. and Sat.)

- **Oak Creek Vineyards**
  (1555 Page Springs Rd., 928/649-0290, www.oakcreekvineyards.net, 10 A.M.-6 P.M. daily)

- **Page Springs Cellars**
  (1500 N. Page Springs Rd., 928/639-3004, www.pagespringscellars.com, 11 A.M.-6 P.M. Sun.-Thurs., till 9 P.M. Fri.-Sat.)

OLD TOWN COTTONWOOD

- **Arizona Stronghold**
  (1023 N. Main St., 928/639-2789, www.azstronghold.com, noon-7 P.M. daily, till 9 P.M. Fri.-Sat.)

- **Burning Tree Cellars**
  (1040 N. Main St., 928/649-8733, noon-9 P.M. daily)

- **Pillsbury**
  (1012 N. Main St., 928/639-0646, www.pillsburywine.com, 11 A.M.-6 P.M. Mon.-Thurs., 11 A.M.-9 P.M. Fri-Sat., noon-6 P.M. Sun.)

- **The Vineyard Wine Bar and Shop**
  (1001 N. Main St., 928/634-2440, www.thevineyardbistro.com, 11 A.M.-11 P.M. Tues.-Sun., later on weekends)

- **The Wine Cellar**
  (1029 N. Main St., 928/649-0444, noon-9 P.M. daily)

JEROME

- **Bitter Creek Winery**
  (240 Hull Ave., 928/634-7033, bittercreekwinery.com, 11 A.M.-5 P.M. Sun.-Fri., 10 A.M.-6 P.M. Sat., hours vary seasonally)

- **Caduceus Cellars**
  (158 Main St., 928/634-3444, www.caduceus.org, 11 A.M.-6 P.M. Sun.-Thurs., 11 A.M.-8 P.M. Fri.-Sat.)

- **Jerome Winery**
  (403 Clark St., 928/639-9067, www.jeromewinery.com, noon-5 P.M. Sun.-Thurs., noon-6 P.M. Fri., 11 A.M.-6 P.M. Sat.)

BETWEEN COTTONWOOD AND CAMP VERDE

- **Alcantara Vineyard**
  (3445 S. Grapevine Way, 928/649-8463, www.alcantaravineyard.com, 11 A.M.-5 P.M. daily)

SEDONA

- **The Art of Wine**
  (101 N. State Route 89A, #B-9, 877/903-9463, www.artowine.com, 10 A.M.-6 P.M. Mon.-Wed., 10 A.M.-8 P.M. Thurs.-Sun.)

WEST SEDONA
American

Follow Airport Road to its end at the very top of the mesa, where you'll see red-rock panoramas and the soaring roofline of the contemporary **Mesa Grill** (1185 Airport Rd. 928/282-2400, http://mesagrillsedona.com, 7 A.M.–9 P.M. daily, $15–30). Plane buffs can keep an eye on the runway while dining on gourmet burgers, pasta, steak, or seafood.

The seasonal menu at ◖ **Heartline Café** (1610 W. State Route 89A, 928/282-0785, http://heartlinecafe.com, 4:30–10 P.M. daily, $15–32) combines Southwestern flavors and Asian touches with a dash of continental flair. Small plates and entrées at this longtime local favorite include sweet potato–corn chowder, tea-smoked chicken dumplings, and daily pasta and fish specials. The dining room has a casual elegance, and the trellised patio is especially lovely. For breakfast or lunch, head next door to **Heartline Gourmet Express** (928/282-3365, 8 A.M.–4 P.M. daily, $15–32), where choices include crab Benedict, lemon-crème stuffed French toast, and a Southwestern wrap, as well as a selection of salads and sandwiches.

To find the **Red Planet Diner** (1655 W. State Route 89A, 928/282-6070, www.redplanet-diner.net, 10 A.M.–11 P.M. daily, $8–18), just look for the UFO out front. Inside you'll find a 1950s-diner-meets-outer-space motif complete with burgers, fries, and old-fashioned malts and shakes. The menu also includes hearty breakfasts and salads, and dinner entrées like steak or vegetarian lasagna.

It's easy to guess the most popular menu item at **Bodacious Burgers** (1950 State Route 89A, 928/282-2255, 11 A.M.–9 P.M. daily, $7–20), but you'll also find an extensive soup-and-salad bar, sandwiches, and other comfort-food classics from meatloaf to prime rib.

If you're looking for a classic small-town diner, head for **Café Jose** (2370 W. State Route 89A, 928/282-0299, http://sedonacafejose. com, breakfast, lunch, and dinner, daily, $5–12) in the Safeway shopping center. Check the whiteboard near the entry for daily specials like chicken and dumplings or pot roast, or order from the varied menu of sandwiches, salads, pastas, and Southwestern entrées. The service is always friendly and, if you're counting pennies, one of the hearty Mexican-style breakfasts is enough to fuel an all-day hike.

Asian

The **Szechuan Restaurant** (1350 W. State Route 89A, 928/282-9288, http://szechuansedona.net, lunch and dinner daily, $11–20) combines Chinese dishes with sushi selections and the popular Martini Bar. Dine in, enjoy the beautiful patio and nightly entertainment, or call ahead for takeout.

For inexpensive sushi, look for **Hiro's** (1730 W. State Route 89A, 928/226-8030, lunch and dinner daily, $5–20), tucked into a small storefront along the highway. Fresh and tasty bento boxes, teriyaki, tempura, and other traditional Japanese favorites round out the menu.

Wild Orchid (2611 W. State Route 89A, 928/282-4422, http://thewildorchidrestaurant. com, lunch and dinner Mon.–Sat., $23–41) features a pan-Asian menu, with choices that include roti, salads, curries, noodles, and teriyaki.

At **Thai Spices** (2986 W. State Route 89A, 928/282-0599, www.thaispices.com, 11:30 A.M.–9 P.M. Mon.–Sat., $10–14), a favorite among local vegetarians, meat eaters can add chicken, beef, or shrimp to most entrées, which include hot noodle dishes, sautées, and flavorful soups and curries. The inexpensive lunch specials are a big hit, and for guests who reserve a day ahead, owner Pearl Black will prepare a platter of macrobiotic selections.

Breakfast and Lunch

In a building once owned by actress Jane Russell, who filmed *Outlaw* in Sedona, **Coffee Pot Restaurant** (2050 W. State Route 89A,

928/282-6626, www.coffeepotsedona.com, 6 A.M.–2 P.M. daily, $5–10) boasts 101 omelets. (But does anyone ever really order the PB&J omelet?) You'll find all-day breakfast favorites, including fluffy pancakes and waffles, and hearty Western-style Mexican fare from huevos rancheros to chimichangas. The dining room is lively and friendly, and when weather permits, you can sit in the spacious enclosed patio in back.

New Frontiers Natural Foods (1420 W. State Route 89A, 928/282-6311, http://new-frontiersmarket.com, 8 A.M.–9 P.M. Mon.–Sat., 8 A.M.–8 P.M. Sun.) is a good spot to pick up supplies for a picnic. The deli offers lots of choices, with seating indoors or on the patio, where you can watch Sedona's health-conscious crowd come to shop, network, or get a chair massage. The grocery side has an impressive selection of organic produce, naturally raised meats, fresh breads, and gourmet cheeses.

Indian

For a touch of the exotic, head for **India Palace** (1910 W. State Route 89A, 928/204-2300, lunch and dinner daily, $5–10). The plentiful lunch buffet is a great value, served with delightfully tender-crisp *naan* (bread) hot from the tandoori oven. Or order from the menu of tandoori-roasted meats, seafood, and curries that can be prepared spicy or not, to your taste. Colorful wall murals provide a rich backdrop for the richly flavored cuisine.

Italian

Dahl & Di Luca Ristorante (2321 W. State Route 89A, 928/282-5219, http://dahlanddiluca.com, 5–10 P.M. daily, $13–33) is always packed with appreciative diners, locals and visitors alike. Start with the extensive antipasti menu, which includes classic bruschetta, polenta parmigiana, or crisp calamari, but leave room for the decadent pastas and grilled meats. If the dining room's over-the-top Tuscan decor isn't your thing, you'll find live music and a lively atmosphere in the bar.

Modern-but-casual **Picazzo's** (1855 W. State Route 89A, 928/282-4140, http://picazzos.com, 11 A.M.–9 P.M. Sun.–Thurs., 11 A.M.–10 P.M. Fri.–Sat., $11–26) epic menu ranges from the meaty (sausage, pepperoni, Canadian bacon) to the cheesy (ricotta, parmesan, mozzarella) to the spicy (chipotle sauce, chorizo, fresh jalapeños) to the gourmet (applewood-smoked bacon, Thai chicken, goat cheese). Crusts include whole grain and gluten-free options, with salads and pastas rounding out the menu.

One of the most delightful (and hidden) patios in Sedona is tucked behind **Apizza Heaven** (2675 W. State Route 89A, 928/282-0519, www.apizzaheavenaz.com, lunch and dinner daily, $10–30), where you can linger over a glass of wine or beer and listen to live music under the stars. It's hard to look beyond the delicious pizza selections, but pastas, calzones, and sandwiches are also on the menu. The hours can be erratic, and it's a bit challenging to find (look for the red sign south of the highway), but once you're here, you'll feel instantly at home.

Mexican and Southwestern

The tiny **Tortas de Fuego** (1630 W. State Route 89A, 928/282-0226, lunch and dinner daily, less than $10) serves salads, tacos, menudo, and the eponymous tortas—hearty Norteño-style sandwiches. The salsa bar has an array of fresh, flavorful concoctions from pico de gallo to pineapple. Don't be discouraged by the lack of parking spaces in front—pull around back where there's room for a few cars.

Barking Frog Grille (2620 W. State Route 89A, 928/204-2000, www.barkingfroggrille.com, 5–10 P.M. daily, $14–30) serves Southwestern favorites that don't seem tired or dated. Kick off happy hour with a prickly pear mojito and stay for dinner to enjoy the crab tacos, pork-belly carnitas, or baby back ribs. Conclude the night with the tequila-laced crème brûlée.

Vegetarian

Raw foodists, here's your Eden. **ChocolaTree** (1595 W. State Route 89A, 928/282-2997, http://chocolatree.com, 9 A.M.–9 P.M. daily) is a confectionery and restaurant serving a mostly raw, 100 percent organic, and all-vegetarian menu. Vibrant soups, spring rolls, sandwiches, and wraps are beautifully prepared, incorporating ingredients grown in the on-site garden. There's also an extensive list of teas, smoothies, wheatgrass shakes, and healing herbal concoctions, as well as the signature handmade chocolates sweetened with agave syrup or honey.

VILLAGE OF OAK CREEK
American

For delicious, no-fuss steak sandwiches and Reubens, join the locals at **PJ's Village Pub & Sports Lounge** (40 W. Cortez Dr., 928/284-2250, www.pjsvillagepub.com, 10 A.M.–2 A.M. daily, $8–14). You'll see bikers, hikers, and golfers huddled around the closely packed tables or at the bar. The tavern is known for its nightly specials like Taco Tuesdays and Baby Back Rib Wednesdays, and the Friday night fish fry has become a weekly VOC ritual.

At the **Marketplace Café** (6645 State Route 179, 928/284-5478, www.mpcsedona.com, 11 A.M.–9 P.M. Sun.–Thurs., till 10 P.M. Fri.–Sat., $8–26), you're likely to find live music, along with a wide-ranging menu of appetizers, hearty salads, seafood, steak, pasta, and pizza. Nightly happy hour specials and a Sunday jazz brunch help keep things lively.

Breakfast and Lunch

Breakfast is served all day at **Miley's Café** (7000 State Route 179, 928/284-4123, 7 A.M.–8 P.M. daily, $6–15) in the Tequa shopping center. This cross between a small-town dinner and a Mexican restaurant serves healthful omelets, huevos rancheros, short stacks and waffles, as well as a diverse lunch and dinner lineup: fish

and chips, burgers, and vegetarian dishes, along with burritos, enchiladas, and carne asada.

Hidden away in a small strip center, the down-home **Blue Moon Café** (6101 State Route 179, 928/284-1831, http://bluemoon-cafe.us, 7 A.M.–9 P.M. daily, $6–10) is a great way to fuel up before a hike or round of golf or refuel afterward on hearty Philly sandwiches, subs, burgers, and hand-tossed pizzas. You'll also find a few Southwestern specialties and a decent beer and wine list.

For coffee drinks, granola, and delectable pastries, look to **Desert Flour** (6446 State Route 179, 928/284-4633, 7 A.M.–3 P.M. Mon., 7 A.M.–8 P.M. Tues.–Sat., 8 A.M.–2 P.M. Sun., $5–12). Heartier breakfasts are also available, and the lunch and dinner menus include wood-fired pizza and generous sandwiches, perfect for a picnic on the red rocks.

It may be a bit off the beaten track, but the **Red Rock Café** (100 Verde Valley School Rd., 928/284-1441, 6:30 A.M.–3 P.M. daily, $6–13) gets praise for its "eggs-ceptional" breakfast menu. For lunch, there's a long list of sandwiches and refreshing salads.

Italian

Award-winning █ **Cucina Rustica Dahl & Di Luca** (7000 State Route 179, 928/284-3010, http://cucinarustica.com, 5–11 P.M. daily, $13–30) offers an elegant, romantic ambience. The salads, soups, and meat dishes are delicious, but it's the fresh, homemade pasta that has made the restaurant a hit with Sedona diners. Eat on the patio or have a seat in the dining room, which features a twinkling, starry sky mural.

Grab a sub or a slice and wash it down with a microbrew at **Famous Pizza** (25 Bell Rock Plaza, 928/284-3805, www.azfamouspizza.com, 11 A.M.–9 P.M. Sun.–Thurs., till 10 P.M. Fri.–Sat., $3–15). The hole-in-the-wall joint serves pies with flaky thin crust, and adds a few pasta dishes for dinner.

Information and Services

TOURIST INFORMATION

Be wary of signs offering travel information. Many are fronts for local time-share companies, and as a trade-off for picking up a handful of brochures, you may be subjected to a hard-sell spiel. (Conversely, you can also land some genuine lodging bargains with coupons for local restaurants and tours if you are willing to sign up for a sales presentation.)

The main official visitor center is staffed by Coconino National Forest and the **Sedona Chamber of Commerce** (1 Forest Rd., 928/282-7722 or 800/288-7336, www.visitsedona.com, 8:30 A.M.–5 P.M. Mon.–Sat., 8 A.M.–3 P.M. Sun.). The convenient Uptown office supplies visitors with maps, directions, and suggestions for choosing the best trail or making the most of your time.

The forest service's **Red Rock Visitor Center** (8375 State Route 179, 928/203-7500, www.redrockcountry.org, 8 A.M.–5 P.M. daily), located just south of the Village of Oak Creek, has exhibits and a small retail area with fun nature-themed gifts, as well as books and maps. The expansive veranda out front is a great spot to snap a panorama of Bell Rock and Courthouse Butte. Two smaller contact stations are staffed seasonally in Oak Creek Canyon. At any of these locations (as well as at businesses in town and a few trailhead vending machines), you can pick up a **Red Rock Pass** ($5 day, $15/week), required for parking at some forest service trailheads.

LIBRARIES

The **Sedona Public Library** (3250 White Bear Rd., 928/282-7714, www.sedonalibrary.org, 10 A.M.–6 P.M. Mon.–Thurs., 10 A.M.–5 P.M. Fri.–Sat.) is a pleasant, light-filled space (by the local architectural firm Design Group) with computers for public use. A smaller branch, **SPL In the Village** (56 W. Cortez Dr., 928/284-1603, www.sedonalibrary.org, 1–5 P.M. Mon.–Fri., 9 A.M.–1 P.M. Sat.), serves the Village of Oak Creek.

HOSPITALS AND EMERGENCY SERVICES

The **Verde Valley Medical Center's Sedona Campus** (3700 W. Highway 89A, 928/204-4100, www.verdevalleymedicalcenter.com) offers 24-hour emergency services in West Sedona, as well as specialty health care. It's a part of Northern Arizona Healthcare, the nonprofit group that includes Cottonwood's Verde Valley Medical Center and Flagstaff Medical Center, the nearest sizable hospitals. Nonemergencies can be handled at **Sedona Urgent Care** (2530 W. State Route 89A, 928/203-4813).

Getting There and Around

Sedona is about two hours north of Phoenix via I-17. You can exit the freeway for State Route 260 (exit 289) or State Route 179 (exit 311). The former route passes through Cottonwood and joins State Route 89A for the Dry Creek Scenic Road. The latter follows the Scenic Red Rock Byway between the Village of Oak Creek and Sedona. Whichever route you choose, the views are inspiring.

Sedona is roughly divided into three areas along State Routes 89A and 179: Uptown, the bustling strip of shops along State Route 89A north of its intersection with State Route 179; West Sedona, a quieter, mostly residential section west of the intersection; and the Village of Oak Creek, an unincorporated area of residences, resorts, and shops approximately seven miles south of the intersection en route to I-17.

Almost all of the area's natural attractions, cultural sights, and restaurants can be reached within a 10-minute drive of Uptown. And with so much neck-craning scenery, you won't mind your time behind the wheel, though the weekend traffic, especially during holidays, can test your patience. Use pullouts to let faster traffic pass or to take photos of the monumental rock formations. If you stop to ask for directions, keep in mind that locals call the 89A/179 intersection "the Y" and use it as a reference point.

Having a car will make Sedona sightseeing easier.

AIR

Most likely, you'll fly into **Phoenix Sky Harbor International Airport** (3400 E. Sky Harbor Blvd., 602/273-3300, www.phxsky-harbor.com) and drive the 90 minutes north to Sedona on I-17, exiting on State Route 179. If you don't want to rent a car, the **Sedona-Phoenix Shuttle** (800/448-7988 or 928/282-2066, www.sedona-phoenix-shuttle.com) has van service from Sky Harbor to the Village of Oak Creek and West Sedona for $50 one-way and $90 round-trip.

US Airways flies into Flagstaff's Pulliam Field. The **Sedona Airport** (235 Terminal Dr., 928/282-1046, www.sedonaairport.org) hosts five fixed-wing and helicopter tour companies, charter air services, and a restaurant.

CAR
Rental Cars

To explore Sedona, Red Rock Country, and the Verde Valley, you'll need a car. Pick up a rental at Phoenix's Sky Harbor Airport or in Sedona. **Hertz** (3009 W. State Route 89, 928/774-4452, www.hertz.com) and **Enterprise** (2090 W. State Route 89A,

928/282-2052, www.enterprise,com) have rental centers in West Sedona. At the Sedona airport terminal, **Discount Rent-a-Car** (877/467-8578) offers hourly rentals in addition to standard rates.

To reach remote trailheads or explore along rocky forest roads, you may want to consider renting a vehicle with four-wheel drive. Jeep rental companies like **Barlow's** (3009 W. State Route 89A, 928/282-4344 or 888/928-5337), located next to Hertz, will provide maps and information about 4WD trails.

Other Transportation

Though it's easy to get around town in your own vehicle, if you prefer to have someone else introduce you to the sights, the **Sedona Trolley** (276 State Route 89A, 928/282-4211, www.sedonatrolley.com, $12 adults, children under 12 free) has two routes that give riders a narrated overview of the town's layout and vistas. The **Verde Lynx** (928/282-0938, $2) connects

© KATHLEEN BRYANT

The Sedona Trolley offers both transportation and tours.

Sedona to the Verde Valley community of Cottonwood, making several in-town stops and running until early evening. If you're out late, you can call **Bob's Taxi** (928/282-1234) or hire **White Tie Transportation** (928/203-4500) to usher you around in a limo or luxury SUV.

Vicinity of Sedona

The red rocks are captivating, but there's plenty of notable natural attractions and historic sites outside of Sedona. Within a few minutes of Uptown, you enter leafy Oak Creek Canyon on Arizona's first officially designated scenic highway.

◖ OAK CREEK CANYON

Drive north from Uptown Sedona on State Route 89A to discover one of Arizona's most picturesque byways. The lush green oasis of Oak Creek Canyon makes a pleasant contrast to the red rocks, and the sparkling creek brings out the Huck Finn in everyone. The scenic highway meanders from Sedona to

Flagstaff for 23 miles, taking about an hour to trace the 12-mile-long canyon and climb the steep switchbacks up to the ponderosa forests of "Flag."

Oak Creek Canyon was formed by a geological fault, creating sheer walls that range from 800 to 2,000 feet tall. Numerous springs feed cool, clear Oak Creek, which nurtures riparian species like Arizona sycamores, blackberries, golden columbine, great blue herons, and raccoons. Trailheads, picnic areas, campgrounds, cabins, and lodges help visitors make the most of this delightful recreation area.

J. J. Thompson was the first to settle in the canyon, arriving on the spot he named Indian

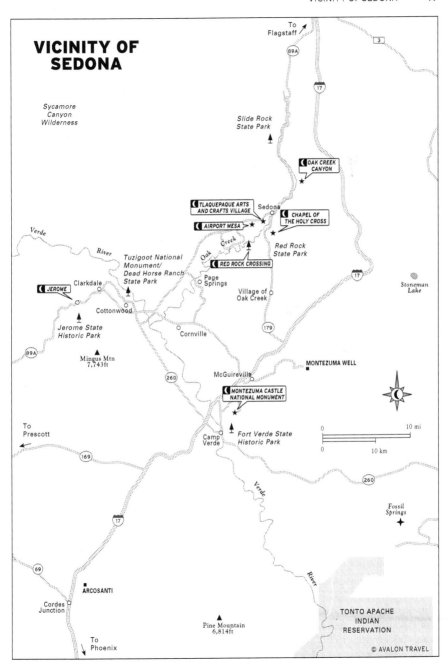

VICINITY OF SEDONA

Sycamore Canyon Wilderness

To Flagstaff

89A

3

17

Slide Rock State Park

OAK CREEK CANYON

TLAQUEPAQUE ARTS AND CRAFTS VILLAGE

Sedona

CHAPEL OF THE HOLY CROSS

AIRPORT MESA

Verde

River

Oak   Creek

Tuzigoot National Monument/ Dead Horse Ranch State Park

Red Rock State Park

RED ROCK CROSSING

Page Springs

17

Stoneman Lake

JEROME

Clarkdale

Cottonwood

Village of Oak Creek

Jerome State Historic Park

Cornville

179

89A

Mingus Mtn 7,743ft

260

McGuireville

MONTEZUMA WELL

MONTEZUMA CASTLE NATIONAL MONUMENT

To Prescott

Camp Verde

Fort Verde State Historic Park

0   10 mi

0   10 km

169

260

17

Fossil Springs

69

Verde

River

ARCOSANTI

Cordes Junction

TONTO APACHE INDIAN RESERVATION

To Phoenix

Pine Mountain 6,814ft

© AVALON TRAVEL

© KATHLEEN BRYANT

Oak Creek's spring-fed waters attract swimmers and anglers.

spot for a picnic or a splash in the creek. Be respectful of private property, as homeowners share space with Coconino National Forest and Slide Rock State Park.

Oak Creek Vista

For an overview of Oak Creek Canyon, stop at the vista (8:30 A.M.–4:30 P.M. daily) located at the top of the switchbacks roughly halfway between Sedona and Flagstaff. This pretty spot in the ponderosa forest is one of the oldest roadside rest areas in the united States. There's a forest service contact station here, where you can pick up books and maps. Most days, weather permitting, Navajo artisans and their families sell items at an arts-and-crafts market.

Slide Rock State Park

When the temperatures start to climb in late spring, the cool waters of Oak Creek beckon. Take the plunge at Slide Rock State Park (6871 N. State Route 89A, 928/282-3034, www.az-stateparks.com, 8 A.M.–7 P.M. daily May–Sept., 8 A.M.–5 P.M. daily Oct.–April, $20 per vehicle), situated seven miles north of Sedona and home to an 80-foot-long natural rock slide, carved into sandstone and basalt bedrock by Oak Creek. The spring-fed water can be a little brisk, and the ride can be a little rough, so be sure to bring water shoes or old sneakers. For a more relaxed experience, wade and splash in an eroded basin or sunbathe like a lizard on a slickrock "beach." The **Slide Rock Market** sells snacks and water, though you may want to bring a picnic and cooler if you plan to stay the day.

Like any well-loved attraction, Slide Rock has become too popular for its own good in recent years. Families from Phoenix and across Arizona descend upon the park on weekends and during holidays in the summer, causing temporary closings when the parking lots fill up or when daily water tests reveals high levels of *E. coli* bacteria. In the fall and winter,

Gardens in 1876. Hollywood came in 1923 to film Zane Grey's popular tale, *Call of the Canyon.* The romantic setting can be visited at Call of the Canyon Day-Use Area, the site of the former Mayhew's Lodge (where some say Grey got his inspiration), and the iconic West Fork Trail. Through the intervening decades, the canyon was a shady sanctuary of motor lodges and camps, and the retreat atmosphere lingers today.

Oak Creek Canyon continues to be a place of rest and relaxation—though you won't escape the crowds, especially in summer when a parade of vehicles cruise the highway looking for campsites or parking spots near popular swimming holes. Fall attracts leaf-peepers when the creek becomes a golden band of sycamores and cottonwoods, punctuated by red splashes of bigtooth maples and set off by evergreen oaks, junipers, and ponderosa pines. No matter the time of year, it's possible to find a quiet the park can be blissfully quiet, providing a nice opportunity to go on a ranger-led nature walk or explore the historic buildings and apple orchard that once belonged to the Pendley family.

Hiking

There are plenty of good hiking trails in Oak Creek Canyon, but the **West Fork Trail** is by far the most popular, and for good reason. The trail follows a tributary canyon for an enchanting Eden of golden columbine, red and yellow monkey flowers, canyon wrens, and redstarts. Tall trees and high canyon walls provide lots of shade—blissful relief during the hot summer. Even first-time hikers will enjoy the easy trail. The canyon's small stream braids over bedrock or collects in reflective pools, easy to wade through or walk around. Most visitors turn around at the three-mile point or sooner for a delightful day hike.

Serious explorers, though, can penetrate even farther into the deep, forested canyon, where they'll need to wade into the creek—and even swim in some spots. The vegetation gets thicker and the trail less defined. It takes a full day to make the additional 11 miles; overnight camping is allowed beyond the first six miles. You must notify rangers if you are planning to backpack overnight.

To get to the trailhead, take State Route 89A past milepost 385 to the **Call of the Canyon Recreation Area** (8 A.M.–8 P.M. Memorial Day–Labor Day, till dusk otherwise, $9), named after Zane Grey's classic Western novel. The trail begins in a small meadow along Oak Creek, passing by the ruins of historic Mayhew's Lodge as it slices into the tributary slot formed by West Fork. You'll find a half-dozen picnic tables near the parking area, which also provides access to the Thomas Point Trail (two miles round-trip), a less-trafficked alternative that climbs the opposite side of Oak Creek Canyon.

Shopping

Two venerable trading posts are located in Oak Creek Canyon. Four miles north of Uptown Sedona, at **Garland's Indian Jewelry** (3953 N. State Route 89A, 928/282-6632, www.garlandsjewelry.com, 10 A.M.–5 P.M. daily), you'll see walls of silver-and-leather concho belts, baskets, kachina carvings, and jewelry. The store sells traditional pieces as well as stunningly modern designs by emerging artisans from Hopi, Navajo, and Zuni tribes.

For more than 60 years, **Hoel's Indian Shop** (9589 N. State Route 89A, 928/282-3925, www.hoelsindianshop.com, 9:30 A.M.–5 P.M. daily) has bought directly from Native artisans, and their first-rate inventory is a testament to this tradition, encompassing jewelry, kachina carvings, pottery, baskets, intricate beadwork, fetishes, and Navajo rugs and blankets. The store is located about 10 miles north of Sedona, and it's a good idea to call first to make sure the doors will be open.

Accommodations

Tucked into the forest along the creek, **Briar Patch Inn** (3190 N. State Route 89A, 928/282-2342, www.briarpatchinn.com, $220–295 d) has 19 cabin-like rooms furnished with rustic wood tables, big beds, old rocking chairs, and brightly colored Native American blankets and rugs, all lovingly cared for by the incredibly friendly and hardworking staff. The accommodations range from quaint one-room hideaways to the sprawling four-bedroom Ponderosa cabin, which is large enough to accommodate 20 people. There are only three TVs on the property, but you can fish for trout, jump into the private swimming hole during the summer, or take a creekside yoga class in the morning before enjoying the buffet breakfast.

Small and pleasantly rustic, **Canyon Wren Cabins** (6425 N. State Route 89A, 928/282-6900, www.canyonwrencabins.com, $155–175 d) has three chalet-styled cedar cabins designed to accommodate two people comfortably, with a small living room, kitchen, bath, and wood-burning fireplace downstairs, and an open loft bedroom with queen bed upstairs.

Garland's Oak Creek Lodge (8067 N. State Route 89A, 928/282-3343, www.garlandslodge.com, $255–305 d) blends the romance of a cabin in the woods with all the style of a small resort. The 1908 homestead is a well-kept Arizona secret, though you may have a hard time getting a reservation for one of the 16 cabins. And as at any good summer hideaway, the lodge's on-site restaurant—simply called The Dining Room—will keep you coming back night after night. Breakfast and dinner are included with your stay. The resort is open early April through mid-November and closed on Sunday. If possible, try to book one of the large cabins with a fireplace.

Forest Houses Resort (9275 N. State Route 89A, 928/282-2999, www.foresthousesresort.com, $120–160 d) offers a quirky woodsy escape. The 15 cabins, A-frame homes, and stone cottages are scattered on 20 acres and range in size to accommodate 2–10 people. Try to reserve one of the creekside cottages, the charming Rock House, or the arty Studio, a former sculpting workshop that overlooks a grassy meadow.

Within the shelter of Oak Creek Canyon are three **forest service campgrounds** (www.fs.usda.gov/coconino, $18/night). Only the smallest is open year-round; the others close for the winter. Amenities are limited to fire rings or grills, tables, toilets, and drinking water (no hookups), but the pluses are shade, easy creek access, and nearby trails and fishing holes. Cave Springs has coin-operated showers that are open to guests from other campgrounds. Some sites can be reserved in advance (877/444-6777, www.recreation.gov).

Food

For an impromptu creekside picnic, pop into **Garland's Indian Gardens** (3951 N. State Route 89A, 928/282-7702, 10 A.M.–5 P.M. daily). The small deli and market prepares fresh sandwiches, salads, and baked goods, and from the grocery you can add lunchtime essentials like water, soda, and chips, as well as locally grown apples and fresh juice. Take your selections to the lovely shady patio in back, or sit out front and watch traffic parade by.

The elegant dining room at **Garland's Oak Creek Lodge** (8067 N. State Route 89A, 928/282-3343, $40 per person) serves up a shared culinary experience. A prix fixe menu of seasonal gourmet delights is presented nightly. Lodge guests and other diners sit at communal tables for a convivial atmosphere. Cocktails are served at 6 P.M. by the fire or out on the lawn, depending on weather, and the dinner bell rings at 7 P.M. The restaurant is open early April through mid-November and closed on Sundays; reservations are required.

PICNIC AREAS

Just north of Sedona on the other side of **Midgely Bridge,** you'll spot a paved parking area. You can walk underneath the bridge for views of Oak Creek Canyon or hike the Huckaby Trail (five miles round-trip) or Wilson Canyon Trail (three miles round-trip). The challenging Wilson Mountain Trail (11 miles round-trip) also begins here.

Two miles north of Uptown, you'll find **Grasshopper Point** (928/203-2900, 8 A.M.–8 P.M. Memorial Day–Labor Day, till dusk otherwise, $8/vehicle), a popular swimming hole and picnic area. In the summer, be sure to arrive early, as the deep pool attracts crowds of cliff-jumpers on weekends. If you're seeking a little solitude, you can stroll along the pleasant Allen's Bend Trail (one mile round-trip).

The heart of Oak Creek Canyon shelters numerous forest service campgrounds and picnic areas. Most day-use sites are open from

8 A.M.–8 P.M. Memorial Day–Labor Day, and till dusk the rest of the year. All require a Red Rock Pass ($5/day, $15/week), available in Sedona, at the contact station near Indian Gardens, or from on-site vending machines.

Encinoso Picnic Area, five miles north of Uptown, has a dozen picnic tables, cooking grills, and lots of elbow room. The North Wilson Trail (11 miles round-trip, strenuous) begins here.

About seven miles north of Uptown, the shady **Halfway Picnic Site** has parking for eight cars and picnic sites above sparkling Oak Creek.

Just a bit farther up the canyon you'll find **Banjo Bill Picnic Area,** a delightful spot with 12 picnic tables and grills.

Bootlegger Picnic Area is a creekside haven nine miles north of Uptown, with a popular fishing hole in addition to picnic tables and grills. The steep and challenging A.B. Young Trail (six miles round-trip) leaves from the south end of the picnic grounds.

Getting There

Oak Creek Canyon may be one of the easiest day trips you've ever taken. Simply head north of Uptown Sedona on State Route 89A; in minutes, you'll be wending your way through one of Arizona's most beautiful wooded canyons, with roadside views of red-rock formations and cool, running waters. Slide Rock State Park is less than 20 minutes from Sedona, and in another 30 minutes or so, you can reach the mountain town of Flagstaff, the unofficial capital of northern Arizona.

Jerome and the Verde Valley

When Spanish explorers first rode into this part of central Arizona in the 16th century, the verdant grass reached their horses' bellies and towering cottonwoods lined the banks of the river. The conquistadors named the area Verde Valley, a testament to its contrast with the Sonoran Desert lands they had just traveled.

The Sinagua people had known of this temperate oasis for hundreds of years, making their homes in pit houses, cliff dwellings, and hilltop pueblos until they moved on around A.D. 1400. By the late 19th century, Anglo settlers arrived and clashed with the Yavapai and Apache bands who roamed the land, prompting the army's intervention. In their zeal to appease the settlers, though, Fort Verde's civilian and military commanders changed the landscape forever. Local pioneers took full advantage of the Native Americans' relocation to reservations by moving more cattle onto the land to supply military encampments and mining towns. The booming mining industry further impacted the hills and valley, forcing many farmers to relocate in the early 1900s. Over time, the waist-high grasses that gave the Verde Valley its name disappeared, and topsoil washed away. Today low grasses, cacti, creosote, and mesquite bosques dominate the landscape.

And yet visitors will find rich reminders of the Verde Valley's dramatic history and natural diversity. Montezuma Castle and Tuzigoot national monuments preserve fascinating prehistoric Sinagua villages. Dead Horse Ranch State Park and the Verde River Greenway enclose a lush riparian reserve near Cottonwood. And for a taste of what life was really like in the Old West, explore the haunted mining town of Jerome or the frontier military installation at Fort Verde.

◖ JEROME

Jerome is a rough-and-tumble town with a colorful history and a penchant for surviving disaster. Once dubbed the "Wickedest Town in

© KATHLEEN BRYANT

The Verde Valley is home to vineyards, orchards, and markets.

the West," the hillside community has endured the ravages of fire, landslides, and an influenza epidemic—not to mention Prohibition and the boom-and-bust business of mining.

Despite its small, walkable size, Jerome packs a whole lot of history. The town was founded in 1876 after prospectors Angus McKinnon and M. A. Ruffner filed the first mining claims. In 1888, entrepreneur William Andrews Clark bought the United Verde Copper Company for $80,000. It became the richest individually owned mine in the world, and Clark made a fortune. Workers arrived in droves, and the city became a melting pot of cultures, with Irish, Greek, and Chinese immigrants showing up in search of jobs and opportunity. In 1912 James "Rawhide" Douglas purchased the UV extension, another bonanza mine that became known as the Little Daisy.

In its heyday, the city's population topped 15,000. Mine owners, engineers, and company

surgeons lived in elegant hillside homes. Saloons, opium dens, and brothels lined back alleys and mountainside gulches. Jerome flourished for decades, but after more than $1 billion had been unearthed from the mines, the bust came to town. The mines closed for good in 1953, and Jerome's population plummeted to about 50 (not counting ghosts). In the 1970s, settlers started to return, but this time they were hippies and artists who found the quaint atmosphere and cheap rent appealing.

Small shops, bars, and hotels still cling to the side of Cleopatra Hill, though today they mainly cater to tourists who are drawn to the town's artsy, quirky, colorful vibe. The past is always present in Jerome's winding streets and historic buildings, and some say literally so. The town is rumored to be haunted by an assortment of ghosts, including Jennie Banters, the former madam who was said to be the wealthiest woman in northern Arizona. Murdered by an opium-addicted boyfriend in 1905, Banters was regarded benevolently by Jeromites—at least in part because she was often the first to rebuild after the repeated fires that often consumed local businesses.

Plan to spend a couple of hours in Jerome, a National Historic Landmark. Explore the narrow streets and intriguing stairways that climb the town's steep slopes. Pop into its galleries and stores, pausing to read the plaques describing historic buildings and adjacent alleyways. It's entertaining to imagine what daily life here must have been like, and how it would have varied according to social standing and livelihood.

Sights
MINE MUSEUM
The local historical society operates the Mine Museum (200 Main St., 928/634-5477, www.jeromehistoricalsociety.com, 9 A.M.–5 P.M. daily, adults $2, children free) in a small storefront. Belying its size, the museum is

© KATHLEEN BRYANT

Take a side trip to Jerome for a day filled with art, history, and shopping.

where there are picnic tables with sweeping views of the Verde Valley and the red rocks beyond. To get to the mansion, look for the brown information sign on your right as you enter town on State Route 89A. You will fork right at Douglas Road just after crossing The Hogback, a narrow ridge with houses on both sides of the highway.

Entertainment and Events

When you're ready for a break, rub elbows with the locals at **The Spirit Room** (166 Main St., 928/634-8809, www.spiritroom. com, 11 A.M.–1 A.M. daily). Beers, bands, and bikes abound at this Jerome watering hole on the main floor of the restored 1898 Connor Hotel. To find it, just look for the line of Harleys parked outside or follow the sound of live music.

If you have a yen for something more refined, visit one of Jerome's three wine-tasting rooms, or time your visit for the **First Saturday Artwalk** (www.jeromeartwalk.com), when artists open their studios, galleries host receptions, and restaurants stay open late. A free shuttle runs 5–8 P.M. to help visitors navigate the hilly streets.

In May, Arizona's oldest **annual home tour** (www.jeromechamber.com) gives visitors an intriguing behind-the-scenes look at a select group of Jerome's historic gems, many of them private residences. And if you're visiting in late October, the community center known as **Spook Hall** (260 Hull Ave.) hosts the Verde Valley's biggest Halloween party, with live music and a costume contest. (Is it any surprise that a town haunted by ghosts lets it all hang out on Halloween?)

Shopping

Jerome's shops and galleries sell everything from kitschy souvenirs to fine art, and the buildings themselves have fascinating tales to tell. Jennie Banters's old brothel is now the home of **Nellie**

jam-packed with information. Exhibitions trace the complex hierarchy of prostitutes, immigrants, and shopkeepers who made their home in Jerome, and the displays of rusty old tools quickly school onlookers in the rigors of life in the mines.

JEROME STATE HISTORIC PARK

For a look at how the other half lived, visit the Jerome State Historic Park (100 Douglas Road, 928/634-5381, http://azstateparks.com, 8:30 A.M.–5 P.M. daily, $5 adult, $2 ages 7–13), housed in the historic Douglas Mansion, a grand home of adobe bricks built in 1916 for the family who owned the Little Daisy Mine. Within the mansion's rooms are period furniture, mineral collections, a fascinating 3-D map of the mining tunnels beneath Jerome, and a small theater showing an entertaining film giving a great overview of Jerome's colorful past. Mining equipment is displayed outside,

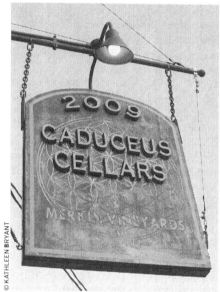

Sample a local wine in one of Jerome's tasting rooms.

Bly (136 Main St., 928/634-0255, http://nellyblyscopes.com, 10 A.M.–5:30 P.M. daily), a small store selling kaleidoscopes, jewelry, and arty gifts. The current incarnation of the **Liberty Theatre** (110 Jerome Ave., 928/649-9016, www.jeromelibertytheater.com), which opened in 1918 and hosted silent films and vaudeville acts, now sells souvenirs and movie memorabilia. A handful of delightfully girly stores sell lingerie, clothing, and jewelry: Ladies, if the menfolk and children get impatient while you browse, send them a mile down Perkinsville Road to the **Gold King Mine** (1000 Perkinsville Road, 928/634-0053, www.goldkingminehosttown.com, 10 A.M.–5 P.M. daily), home to a decades-old collection of mining equipment, vehicles, and other Americana, plus one very friendly burro.

Accommodations

A National Historic Landmark, the haunted **Jerome Grand Hotel** (200 Hill St., 928/634-8200, www.jeromegrandhotel.com, $120–205 d) sits high above town on Cleopatra Hill. The 12-room **Hotel Connor** (164 Main St., 928/634-5006, www.connorhotel.com, $90–165 d), built in 1898, offers respite from the high-spirited happenings in the Spirit Room saloon below.

The town is home to a handful of delightful B&Bs and guest apartments. A sophisticated throwback to Jerome's Victorian past, **The Miner's Cottage** (553 Main St., 928/254-1089, www.theminerscottage.com, $950 per week) has two master suites available for rental by the week. Shorter stays are possible on request. **The Surgeon's House** (100 Hill St., 928/639-1452, www.surgeonshouse.com, $145–195), built in 1916 for the UV mine's chief surgeon, is a gracious retreat with four guest suites and a lovely garden that has views all the way to Sedona's red rocks.

Food

The Asylum Restaurant and Lounge (200 Hill St., 928/639-3197, 11 A.M.–3:30 P.M. and 5–9 P.M. daily, $10–32) at the Jerome Grand Hotel features New American cuisine with a Southwestern twist. Meals are complemented by a terrific view of Verde Valley and an extensive wine list, which gets kudos from *Wine Spectator* magazine.

Mile High Grill & Spirits (309 Main St., 928/634-5094, www.milehighgrillandinn.com, lunch daily, breakfast Thurs.–Mon., dinner Fri.–Sat., $6–17) serves hearty breakfasts, followed by sandwiches, salads, wraps, and burgers for lunch. Weekend dinner entrées include updated classics like meatloaf, hanger steak, drunken shrimp, and salmon with chimichurri sauce.

◖**15.Quince** (363 Main St., 928/634-7087, 11 A.M.–8 P.M. Mon.–Thurs., 11 A.M.–9 P.M. Fri., 9 A.M.–9 P.M. Sat., 9 A.M.–8 P.M. Sun., $8–17) dishes up a lively atmosphere along with

New Mexican cuisine smothered in specialty salsas. Quince's owner/chef Vlad Costa has also reopened the beloved **Flat Iron Café** (416 Main St., 928/634-2733, www.flatironjerome.com, 8:30 A.M.–3 P.M. Wed.–Mon., $4–9), where you'll find breakfasts and lunches with a bit less spice than at Quince but every bit as delicious.

Named for the infamous madam Jennie Banters, **Belgian Jennie's Bordello Bistro & Pizzeria** (412 Main St., 928/639-3141, 11:30 A.M.–8 P.M. Thurs.–Mon.) fixes thin-crust pizzas and hearty pastas like fettuccine alfredo, lobster ravioli, and tortellini carbonara.

Getting There

From Sedona, take State Route 89A west to Cottonwood. You can turn left at the fourth stoplight to stay on State Route 89A (the "cut-off" to Jerome), or opt for a more leisurely drive by staying on Main Street and continuing through Old Town Cottonwood. This route passes Dead Horse Ranch State Park and Tuzigoot National Monument before traveling through the former mining company town of Clarkdale. It rejoins State Route 89A to wind up the side of Cleopatra Hill to Jerome.

COTTONWOOD

Backdropped by the Black Hills, Cottonwood was founded in 1879 along the tree-lined Verde River, becoming home to a half-dozen families who supplied Fort Verde and later the workers from Jerome's mines. By the 1920s, the flourishing commerce center was known as Arizona's "Biggest Little Town" because it had more businesses per capita than any other town in the state.

Now numbering 11,000 residents, Cottonwood still retains plenty of small-town charm, especially along Main Street in Old Town, the central historic district. The meandering path of the Verde, one of Arizona's last free-flowing rivers, is marked by a lush band of green, thanks to the towering cottonwood

© KATHLEEN BRYANT

Wine and dine along Main Street in Old Town Cottonwood.

trees that gave the town its name. And though the community has nurtured its connections to the past, modern Cottonwood also serves as a bedroom community for Sedona workers who can't afford to live in pricy Red Rock Country.

Dead Horse Ranch State Park

To catch a glimpse of what the Verde Valley looked like more than a century ago, head to Dead Horse Ranch State Park (675 Dead Horse Ranch Rd., 928/634-5283, http://azstateparks. com, 8 A.M.–5 P.M. daily, $7/vehicle), a nearly pristine stretch of Verde River that offers camping ($15–55), hiking, mountain biking, fishing, and equestrian areas. Officially classified as a cottonwood and willow riparian gallery forest—one of only 20 such ecosystems left in the world—the 423-acre park protects one of the last stretches of free-running river in the Sonoran Desert and more than 100 species of migrating birds, including the black hawks and golden eagles that come every year to feast on trout. Late in April, the park is home base for the region's premiere nature event, the **Verde Valley Birding and Nature Festival** (www. birdyverde.org), with workshops, exhibits, and field trips exploring the region's diverse habitats.

Look for the park's brown information sign along Main Street, after the road curves to the left (west) and approaches Old Town. Turn right (north) on 10th Street, continuing across the river and turning right on Dead Horse Ranch Road, which leads to the park entrance.

Old Town

Elvis walked here, and so can you. Strolling down Main Street in Old Town Cottonwood is a trip down memory lane, with brick storefronts and quaint signage offering a slice of Americana. Many buildings are undergoing restoration, and in recent years, boutiques and galleries have been joined by wine-tasting rooms and trendy cafés as Cottonwood rediscovers its agricultural roots. The four-block Old Town district (www.oldtown.org) is on the National Register of Historic Places, and the best way to see architectural details like hammered tin ceilings and river-rock masonry is to explore on foot. Three dozen buildings date to the 1920s and 1930s, some of them hiding underground rooms and tunnels used by Prohibition-era bootleggers. The proprietor of the **Cottonwood Hotel** (930 N. Main St., 928/634-9455, www.cottonwoodhotel.com) leads fascinating walking tours for $30–45. Or, for a self-guided nature walk, start at the **Old Jail** (1101 N. Main St.) and head down the mile-long Jail Trail to the Verde River Greenway. Check in at the **Pillsbury Wine Company** (1012 N. Main, 928/639-0646) for brochures and information about things to do in Old Town.

Entertainment and Events

Cottonwood boasts one of the finest concert venues in northern Arizona, the **Old Town Center for the Arts** (5th and Main St., 928/634-0940, www.oldtowncenter.org). Under the direction of musician and luthier William Eaton, OTCA has hosted musicians, comedy, and theater in its renovated historic building.

Housed in a former garage, **The Rendezvous in Old Town** (777 N. Main St., 928/634-3777, http://riotcottonwood.com, 2–9 P.M. Mon.–Thurs., 11 A.M.–midnight Fri.–Sat., 11 A.M.–9 P.M. Sun. $8–13) aka RIOT, keeps things hoppin' late with a small-but-creative fusion menu, two dozen beers on tap, a generous wine list, and nightly entertainment.

Blazin' M Ranch (1875 Mabery Ranch Rd., 928/634-0334, www.blazinm.com, 5–8:30 P.M. daily, closed Jan. and Aug., adults $35, children 3–12 $20) serves up "cowboy vittles, stories, tomfoolery." The dinner bell rings at 6:30, but arrive early to enjoy the full Wild West experience, including a shooting gallery, train ride, and petting zoo. Browse the old-fashioned shops—or dress up as rough-and-tumble cowboys and saloon madams for an "Olde Tyme" photo. Dinner includes barbecued meats, cowboy beans, chunky applesauce, and homemade biscuits. Afterward, the Blazin' M Cowboys carry on the Old West tradition of music and storytelling. Call for reservations.

In early May, the **Verde Valley Fair** (800 E. Cherry St., 928/634-3290, www.verdevalleyfair.com, $3–10) is a classic, with livestock exhibits, a carnival, and plenty of blue-ribbon quilts, jams, and pies. In November, a street fair with food and music, **Walkin' On Main** (928/639-3200), celebrates historic Main Street.

Following the annual **Christmas Parade** held on the first Saturday of December is the much-anticipated **Chocolate Walk** (4–8 P.M.). Participate by taking your chocolate collection bag from store to store, enjoying Christmas decorations and sampling sweet treats into the evening as you browse for holiday gifts. For more information about this and other events, contact the Chamber of Commerce (1010 S. Main St., 928/634-7593, www.cottonwood-chamberaz.org).

Shopping

The Verde Valley's largest commerce center, Cottonwood is home to the familiar big-box stores that don't fit into Jerome or Sedona, as well as many mom-and-pop service businesses. Antiques stores dot the main drag, with most galleries and boutiques centering in Old Town. Among them is **Art Institute Glitter** (712 N. Balboa St., 928/639-0805, www.artglitter.com, 9 A.M.–5 P.M. Mon.–Fri., 10 A.M.–3 P.M. Sat.), a must-stop for scrappers, crafters, and all who like shiny things. The store carries crafting supplies, but the mainstay is glitter, to the tune of 60,000 pounds a year. At **Bent River Books and Music** (1010 N. Main St., 928/634-8332, www.bentriverbm.com, winter hours 10 A.M.–6 P.M. Mon. and Wed.–Sat., noon–5 P.M. Sun.), you can sip a cup of tea and browse new, used, and collectible books and ephemera for hours. The bookstore helps keep Old Town lively with author events and live acoustic music on weekends.

Pick up a bottle of local vino at any of the wine-tasting rooms on Main, and stop at **Orion Bread** (1028 N. Main St., 928/649-1557, www.orionbread.com, 8 A.M.–5 P.M. Mon.–Sat., 7 A.M.–4 P.M. Sun.) for a loaf of Rosemary Italian or Miner's Sourdough and some jumbo cookies. Add olive oil from **Verde Valley Olive Oil Traders** (1002 N. Main St., 928/634-9900, www.vvoliveoil.com, 10:30 A.M.–6 P.M. Mon.–Sat., 11 A.M.–6 P.M. Sun.) to create the perfect picnic.

Accommodations

You'll find a few chain motels in Cottonwood, which makes a convenient base if you're counting pennies or if rooms in Sedona or Jerome are booked. The **Pines Motel** (920 Camino Real, 928/634-9975, www.azpinesmotel.com, $50–90) has clean, bright rooms, and the mini-suites, equipped with full-size refrigerators, are great for larger groups or big families. Offering boutique accommodations in a restored 1925 grocery, **The Tavern Hotel** (904 N. Main, 928/639-1669, http://thetavernhotel.com, $150–170) is a stylish option with amenities that include breakfast vouchers for Old Town cafés.

Food

Willy's Burgers & Shakes (794 N. Main St., 928/634-6648, 11 A.M.–7 P.M. Mon.–Sat., 11 A.M.–3 P.M. Sun., $5–8) recreates the classic diner ambience of the 1950s, right down to the black-and-white checkered floor and swell jukebox. Look for the converted gas station's old pumps at out front, then refuel on classic burgers, gooey grilled cheese sandwiches, and malts or shakes.

Main Street's **Red Rooster** (901 N. Main St., 928/649-8100, http://oldtownredrooster-cafe.com, breakfast and lunch daily, $6–14) puts a gourmet touch on comfort food. The breakfast skillets (and coffee) are especially good; so are the homemade soups and quiche.

Crema Café (917 N. Main St., 928/649-5785, www.cremacafe89a.com, breakfast and lunch daily, $5–10) has a simple menu with a Euro flair. Soups, salads, and sandwiches incorporate local organic ingredients, and the gelatos and sorbets are made from scratch.

Nic's Italian Steak & Crab House (925 N. Main St., 928/634-9626, www.nicsaz.com, diner nightly, $9–17) packs in locals with solid seafood dishes, top-notch steaks, and Italian classics like eggplant parmesan, lasagna, and chicken piccata.

Getting There

From Sedona, take State Route 89A west, which includes 6.5 miles known as the Dry Creek Scenic Road. As you descend toward the Verde Valley, the landscape changes from red-rock buttes and juniper woodland to high-desert chaparral and tawny grasslands. Scan the southern horizon for House Mountain, an extinct volcano with a house-shaped top, named by Cottonwood-area settlers in the 1870s. After you cross the Verde River and enter Cottonwood, the highway becomes Main Street.

TUZIGOOT NATIONAL MONUMENT

Between Old Town Cottonwood and Clarkdale, Tuzigoot National Monument (928/634-5564, www.nps.gov/tuzi, 8 A.M.–5 P.M. daily Sept.–May, 8 A.M.–6 P.M. daily June–Aug., $5 adults, children free) protects a 110-room hilltop pueblo that was once home to Sinagua villagers, who began its construction around A.D. 1100. The three-story pueblo formed an intricate complex of living,

Tuzigoot National Monument

© RANDY MIRAMONTEZ/123RF.COM

cooking, and storage spaces. Visitors can explore rooms up close, and the museum has the area's finest collection of prehistoric artifacts. The largest reconstructed room at the top of the complex has views of the Black Hills, Verde River, and Tavasci Marsh, a landscape that offered a large diversity of minerals, food, fuel, and other resources for the villagers, who traded with communities hundreds of miles away.

Getting There

From Sedona, take State Route 89A west to Cottonwood, where the highway becomes Main Street. Continue on Main Street through Old Town. Look for the turnoff to Tuzigoot Road on the right, marked by a brown information. Follow the road to the park entrance.

CLARKDALE

Below Jerome is the postcard-pretty town of Clarkdale (pop. 3,800), founded in 1912 and constructed almost entirely in one go as the company town for William Clark's UV mine smelter. Considered to be Arizona's first master-planned community, the town boasted cutting-edge technology for its time—telephone, telegraph, electricity, modern plumbing, and sewer. Amenities included a central park with a bandstand, and a handsome Spanish Colonial-style clubhouse with a library, bowling alley, and pool.

Today, the bandstand still hosts evening summertime concerts in the town square, surrounded by a collection of charming bungalows. The townsite is a National Historic District, encompassing 386 homes and businesses. The brick storefronts along Main Street look much the same as they did in 1928 when semiretired lawman Jim Roberts foiled a bank robbery amidst a flurry of bullets.

Find out more about the town's past at the **Clarkdale Historical Society and Museum** (900 1st N., 928/649-1198, http://

clarkdaleheritage.org, 10 A.M.–1 P.M. Wed.–Sun.), where you can pick up a map for a walking tour. The museum also has a gift shop with work by local artists.

Verde Canyon Railroad

Billed as Arizona's "longest-running nature show," the Verde Canyon Railroad (300 N. Broadway, 800/582-7245, http://verdecanyonrr.com, $55–80) leads into a steep-walled limestone canyon sheltering waterfowl and bald eagle nesting sites. Special events include the Grape Train Escape ($120), with first-class seats and wine-tasting on a twilight ride. Or you can rent the entire caboose ($600) for a group up of up to six. Packages with hotel accommodations are available.

Accommodations and Food

For a getaway that feels like home, settle into the **Blue Heron Guest House** (200 Main St., 982/634-3989, www.blueheronaz.com, $85–100), an early 20th-century workshop remodeled into a charming cottage/studio, equipped with a kitchenette. After a day of exploring, you can kick back on the shady front porch or warm up near the outdoor fireplace.

Presiding on Clarkdale's Main Street is **Su Casa** (1000 Main St., 928/634-2771, lunch and dinner daily, $8–16) a popular spot serving relatively tame Mexican fare.

Getting There

From Sedona, take State Route 89A west toward Cottonwood. Turn right (north) onto the Mingus Avenue extension, crossing the Verde River. At the next stoplight, turn right on Main Street, continuing through Old Town and passing Tuzigoot National Monument en route to Clarkdale. A left turn on Clarkdale's Main Street will take you through the town's historic center; staying to the right on Broadway leads to the Verde Canyon Railroad depot.

Visit the local wineries along Page Springs Road.

PAGE SPRINGS AND CORNVILLE

The creekside communities of Page Springs and Cornville are the heart of the Verde Valley's burgeoning agricultural revival. You can travel through both unincorporated areas (with a total population of about 4,500) on a pleasant loop drive from State Route 89A. Five miles of Page Springs Road have been designated by Yavapai County as a historic and scenic route. Cactus-covered hillsides sidle up to acres of lush vineyards as the route passes orchards, farms, wineries, and Cornville's **Windmill Park** (9950 E. Cornville Rd.), a pleasant eight-acre oasis along lower Oak Creek with picnic tables, horseshoes, and a working windmill. You won't see any cornfields in Cornville (the U.S. Postal Service misspelled the town's name, meant to acknowledge a pioneer family named Coan), but you will see creekside pastures.

Birders won't want to miss strolling around the 82-acre **Page Springs Fish Hatchery**

(1600 N. Page Springs Rd., 928/634-4805, 8 A.M.–4 P.M. daily, free), designated an Important Bird Area by the Audobon Society. The hatchery has a nature trail and an interpretive center. As well as trout, native fish species facing extinction in the Grand Canyon's Colorado River are nurtured here.

Accommodations

Lovely and peaceful **Lo Lo Mai Springs Resort** (11505 Lo Lo Mai Rd., 928/634-4700, www. lolomai.com) has shady RV spaces and tent sites (starting at $37) and camping cabins (kitchen needs are provided; towels and bedding are not, $75–140). Some of the cabins include bathrooms. The old-timey resort property along the creek has shower facilities, a seasonal pool and Jacuzzi, a playground, horseshoe pits, and a clubhouse. Though the resort operates on a membership basis, vacancies are often available for nonmembers. It's an ideal spot for a family reunion or large gathering.

Food

After a tasting flight or two at the vineyards along Page Springs Road, you may be ready for a meal nearby. The dining room at **Up the Creek** (1975 N. Page Springs Rd., 928/634-9954, 11 A.M.–9 P.M. Wed.–Sun., $8–30) juts over the lazy waters of lower Oak Creek for a treetop feel. Steaks and barbecue are the specialty, but vegetarians will appreciate the made-from-scratch tomato–sour cream–corn-meal pie.

The aptly named **Harry's Hideaway** (10990 E. Cornville Rd., 928/639-2222, http://harryshideaway.com, lunch and dinner Tues.–Sat., $8–18) may be a little hard to find—it's tucked into a small shopping center near Casey's Corner—but the owners will make you feel like family. The wine-friendly, wide-ranging menu runs the gamut from American comfort food to Mediterranean dishes.

Across the road from Cornville's post office, **Vince's Little Star** (9375 E. Cornville Rd., 928/634-4063, dinner Tues.–Sat., $8–15) is a classic small-town Italian joint, with red-checkered tablecloths, candles in chianti bottles, and Frank and Dean crooning on the stereo. Reservations are recommended.

Getting There

From Sedona, take State Route 89A west toward Cottonwood. Turn left (south) at Page Springs Road. After passing through Page Springs, the road intersects with the Cornville Road at Casey's Corner. Turn right and continue through the village of Cornville where the road loops back toward State Route 89A.

CAMP VERDE

At the end of the Civil War, farmers and ranchers began to settle around the confluence of the Verde River and West Clear Creek, aiming to supply food, cattle, hay, and other goods to the army at Fort Whipple and the growing mining community of Prescott. Historically,

this prime location was used by seminomadic bands of Tonto Apaches and Yavapais for hunting game and gathering wild plants. Finding their traditional lands fenced and plowed, the Indians began raiding the settlers' crops and herds. In early 1865 the U.S. army established Camp Lincoln to deal with the escalating conflict, later moving the camp and renaming it Fort Verde.

Over the next decades, the fort and town became the center of Arizona's Indian Wars, associated with legendary scouts, chiefs, and commanders like General Crook. After the removal of many Yavapais and Apaches in 1875 and the surrender of Geronimo in 1886, the fort was abandoned. Concerned locals who recognized its historical importance joined together in the 1960s to rescue it from further disintegration. Camp Verde, the area's oldest settled community, takes an active role in preserving the past. The local historical society (435 S. Main, 928/567-9560) displays photographs, artifacts, and artwork in their small museum and maintains two historic buildings, the Clear Creek Church and the home of George Hance.

Today, more than 10,000 people live in the modern town of Camp Verde, and many families continue to farm and ranch along the river. February's Pecan and Wine Festival (www.pecanandwinefestival.com) spotlights two local crops, and July's CornFest (http://visitcampverde.com) celebrates a third. The main drag is lined with a few antiques shops and restaurants, and the town serves as the northern gateway to the Tonto National Forest, offering recreational activities from rafting the Verde River to exploring on horseback or by Jeep. The real highlight, however, is being able to step back into the past at this place where so many cultures intersected.

Fort Verde State Historic Park

See the real Old West at Fort Verde (125 E.

Hollamon, 928/567-3275, http://azstateparks. com, 9 A.M.–5 P.M. Thurs.–Mon., $5 adults, $2 ages 7–13), offering a glimpse of a frontier soldier's life during the Indian Wars of the late 1800s. Originally built in 1871, the fort housed as many as 300 soldiers who were stationed here to protect Anglo settlers from Apache and Yavapai raiders. What remains of the fort today is considered the best-preserved example of Indian War–era military architecture in the state.

Three historical houses still stand along the parade ground, decorated with 1880s-period furnishings. The Surgeon's Quarters was home to 27 army doctors over the years, and the downstairs office displays bonesaws and other medical equipment. The other two houses served as quarters for bachelor officers and the fort's commanding officer and his family. The former headquarters building now houses a museum with artifacts and photographs highlighting the soldiers, civilians, and Indian tribes who once lived in the region. Exhibits describe how Yavapai and Apache bands were pursued and incarcerated on a reservation in the Verde Valley, then force-marched to the San Carlos Apache reservation in 1875.

Several times a year, the fort hosts candelit tours, workshops, and other events. Mid-October brings Fort Verde Days, when reenactors representing Buffalo Soldiers (the army's African American cavalry regiments) ride into town.

Verde Valley Archaeology Center

Learn more about the prehistoric Sinagua Indians and the contemporary Yavapai and Apache tribes at the Verde Valley Archaeology Center (345 S. Main, 928/567-0066, www. verdevalleyarchaeology.org, 9:30 A.M.–4 P.M. Thurs.–Fri., 11 A.M.–4 P.M. Sat., noon–4 P.M. Sun., by donation). The volunteer-staffed museum displays artifacts from area sites, and it's a good idea to call first to verify hours. The center's research lab is used by a dedicated group of avocational archaeologists who educate locals and visitors about site preservation and assist professionals in stabilizing, monitoring, and investigating cultural sites from Camp Verde to Sedona. During March, the center hosts events for Arizona Archaeology Month, and in September, it holds a festival of American Indian arts.

Entertainment and Accommodations

Familiar motel and fast-food chains have staked out the freeway interchange at State Route 260. Travelers who want to add a cultural aspect to their visit can exit a couple miles north for **Cliff Castle Casino** (555 W. Middle Verde Rd., 928/567-7900, www.cliffcastle-casinohotel.com), conveniently situated near Montezuma Castle National Monument. The casino, owned by the Yavapai-Apache Nation, offers slots, poker, blackjack, and keno, as well as live entertainment at the outdoor **Stargazer Pavilion** and inside at its nightclub, **Dragonfly Lounge.** The casino has four restaurants (including the casual diner Johnny Rockets and the elegant Storyteller), a bowling alley, and a video arcade. Just downhill, you can find a clean, quiet room at **The Hotel at Cliff Castle** (928/567-6611 or 800/524-6343, $100–120 d).

Getting There

To get to Camp Verde from Sedona, drive south on State Route 179 through the Village of Oak Creek to I-17, where you'll merge right and head southwest. Take exit 287, and turn left onto State Route 260. Turn left to head toward downtown on the Finnie Flats Road, which becomes Main Street. You'll see signs directing you to the fort. If you are driving from Phoenix, drive I-17 north to exit 285, where you'll follow State Route 260 south (also known as the General Crook Trail) to Camp Verde's Main Street.

© KATHLEEN BRYANT

Montezuma Castle National Monument

◖ MONTEZUMA CASTLE NATIONAL MONUMENT

Walking up the shaded creekside path to view Montezuma Castle (I-17 exit 289, 928/567-3322, www.nps.gov/moca, 8 A.M.–5 P.M. daily, 8 A.M.–6 P.M. daily Jun.–Aug., $5 adults, children under 16 free), you can't help but imagine what it must have been like to live in the five-story pueblo, one of the best-preserved cliff dwellings in North America.

Built into a deep recess in the limestone cliff and sheltered from the elements, the 20-room pueblo and nearby Castle A, with 45–50 rooms, were occupied from about A.D. 1250 to the 1400s. Villagers cultivated fields along Beaver Creek and supplemented their diet by hunting and gathering native plants. The pueblos and their rooftop plazas—constructed of stone with wood timbers and mud mortar—were used for sleeping, preparing food, weaving, making pottery, and storing surplus food. The Sinagua participated in a vast trade network that reached as far south as present-day Mexico and as far west as the Pacific.

Explorers who discovered the site in the 1800s speculated (incorrectly) that the Aztecs and their legendary emperor Montezuma built the impressive structure. Museum exhibits inside the visitor center provide an overview of the site, the prehistoric Sinagua culture, and the contemporary Yavapai and Apache people who inhabit the Verde Valley today.

Montezuma Well

The Sinagua were experts at making the most of the Verde Valley's natural resources. Just 11 miles north of Montezuma Castle, you can witness their ingenuity at another of Arizona's natural wonders, Montezuma Well (I-17 exit 293, 928/567-4521, www.nps.gov/moca, 8 A.M.–5 P.M. daily, 8 A.M.–6 P.M. daily Jun.–Aug., $5 adults, children free). Small cliffside ruins and canals are clustered around the site, which provided a vital source of water to the

Sinagua farmers and also figures in Yavapai and Apache creation stories. You can imagine its importance in an area that averages 11 inches of rain annually. Underground springs still feed 1.5 million gallons of water every day into the well, which actually is a large sinkhole, 365 feet across and 55 feet deep. The constant supply of 74-degree water has created an ecosystem with several plants and animals not found anywhere else in the world. Unique species of crustaceans, water scorpions, and turtles thrive in the warm, carbon dioxide–rich water that is inhospitable to most fish and aquatic life. You can walk down to the ruins along the water's edge or to the well's tree-shaded outlet, where the temperature can be as much as 20 degrees cooler than in the surrounding grasslands. Nearby, a ramada protects the remains of a Hohokam-style pit house.

Getting There
From Sedona, head south on State Route 179 to I-17. Take exit 289, drive east through two roundabouts for less than a mile, and then turn left on Montezuma Castle Road. Plenty of signs will make navigating the narrow two-lane road quite easy. From Phoenix, follow I-17 north about an hour and turn right at exit 289, where signs will direct you through two traffic circles to the monument's entrance. To reach Montezuma Well, drive I-17 to exit 293. Follow the signs through the towns of McGuireville and Rimrock to the park's entrance.

OUT OF AFRICA WILDLIFE PARK
Kids love animals, and they'll see plenty of them at Out of Africa Wildlife Park (3505 State Route 260, 928/567-2840, www.outofafricapark.com, 9:30 A.M.–5 P.M. daily, $36 adults, $20 ages 3–12), a 100-acre wildlife refuge with lions, tigers, giraffes, and other exotic beasts. Set aside a half-day for activities like the tiger splash or snake show and tours. Two of the tours use trams or safari vehicles, but you can walk to photo platforms and habitat areas at your own pace as well. There are a snack bar and gift shop on-site, and you'll often find discounted tickets online or at local hotels and businesses.

Getting There
From West Sedona, take State Route 89A to Cottonwood. Turn left on State Route 260 and travel 10 miles to Cherry Road. Turn right on Cherry, then right on Commonwealth Drive, which leads to the park entrance.

ARCOSANTI
Arcosanti (928/632-7135, www.arcosanti.org, 10 A.M.–4 P.M. daily) is a community designed and built by Italian architect Paolo Soleri as the embodiment of his principles of "arcology"— a mixture of architecture and ecology. Soleri's goal was to create a "lean alternative" to the wastefulness of modern cities by making them more compact and self-sustaining. His continuing real-world experiment began in 1970, more than two decades after he came to the Southwest to study with Frank Lloyd Wright at Taliesin West.

Perched on a high desert bluff, Arcosanti today is home to just a few hundred people at any one time. From a distance, it resembles an unlikely combination of Italian hill town and sci-fi movie set. But up close, the handcrafted details and perfectly human scale make this pioneering example of urban sustainability a delight to visit. Guided tours are $10, and special events include live music, art shows, and dinners under the arched concrete vaults, which are open to the desert skies.

Food
If your timing is right, you can join the community for a meal ($9) at the cafeteria, open daily at noon for lunch and reopening at 6 P.M. for dinner. Overnight stays ($40–100)

Sales of wind chimes and bells help fund Arcosanti's projects.

are available with prior arrangement. Special-interest tours and workshops can also be arranged, including weeklong learning programs.

Getting There

From Phoenix, drive north some 60 miles on I-17. Take exit 262 to State Route 69. Turn right on the Cordes Lakes Road. Signs for Arcosanti direct you north over 2.5 miles of unpaved roads to the site.

From Sedona, head south on State Route 179 to I-17. Drive the freeway 36 miles south, taking exit 262A to State Route 69. Turn left on the Cordes Lakes Road and follow the signs.

www.moon.com

MOON.COM is ready to help plan your next trip! Filled with fresh trip ideas and strategies, author interviews, informative travel blogs, a detailed map library, and descriptions of all the Moon guidebooks, Moon.com is all you need to get out and explore the world—or even places in your own backyard. While at Moon.com, sign up for our monthly e-newsletter for updates on new releases, travel tips, and expert advice from our on-the-go Moon authors. As always, when you travel with Moon, expect an experience that is uncommon and truly unique.

KEEP UP WITH MOON ON FACEBOOK AND TWITTER
JOIN THE MOON PHOTO GROUP ON FLICKR

MAP SYMBOLS

▦▦▦	Expressway	☾	Highlight	✗	Airfield	⚲	Golf Course
▦▦▦	Primary Road	○	City/Town	✗	Airport	▯	Parking Area
▬▬	Secondary Road	◉	State Capital	▲	Mountain	▰	Archaeological Site
∙∙∙∙∙∙	Unpaved Road	⊛	National Capital	✦	Unique Natural Feature	▮	Church
- - - -	Trail	★	Point of Interest			▮	Gas Station
∙∙∙∙∙∙∙∙∙	Ferry	•	Accommodation	⬚	Waterfall	◌	Glacier
-×-×-×	Railroad	▾	Restaurant/Bar	▲	Park	◌	Mangrove
▦▦▦	Pedestrian Walkway	▪	Other Location	▯	Trailhead	▨	Reef
▥▥▥	Stairs	⋀	Campground	⚡	Skiing Area	▱	Swamp

CONVERSION TABLES

°C = (°F - 32) / 1.8
°F = (°C x 1.8) + 32
1 inch = 2.54 centimeters (cm)
1 foot = 0.304 meters (m)
1 yard = 0.914 meters
1 mile = 1.6093 kilometers (km)
1 km = 0.6214 miles
1 fathom = 1.8288 m
1 chain = 20.1168 m
1 furlong = 201.168 m
1 acre = 0.4047 hectares
1 sq km = 100 hectares
1 sq mile = 2.59 square km
1 ounce = 28.35 grams
1 pound = 0.4536 kilograms
1 short ton = 0.90718 metric ton
1 short ton = 2,000 pounds
1 long ton = 1.016 metric tons
1 long ton = 2,240 pounds
1 metric ton = 1,000 kilograms
1 quart = 0.94635 liters
1 US gallon = 3.7854 liters
1 Imperial gallon = 4.5459 liters
1 nautical mile = 1.852 km

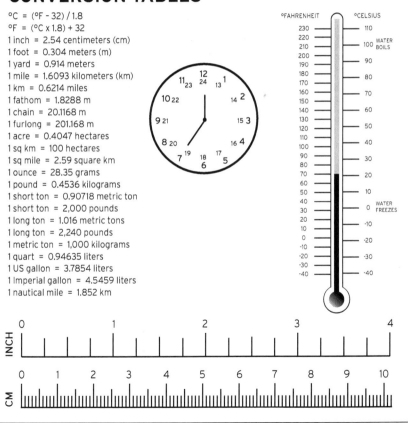

MOON SPOTLIGHT SEDONA

Avalon Travel
a member of the Perseus Books Group
1700 Fourth Street
Berkeley, CA 94710, USA
www.moon.com

Editor: Erin Raber
Series Manager: Kathryn Ettinger
Copy Editor: Ashley Benning
Graphics Coordinator: Elizabeth Jang
Production Coordinator: Elizabeth Jang
Cover Designer: Kathryn Osgood
Map Editor: Albert Angulo
Cartographers: Kaitlin Jaffe, Heather Sparks,
  Andy Butkovic, Chris Henrick

ISBN-13: 978-1-61238-609-6

Text © 2013 by Kathleen Bryant.
Maps © 2013 by Avalon Travel.
All rights reserved.

Jeff Ficker wrote the first edition of *Moon Phoenix, Scottsdale & Sedona*.

Some photos and illustrations are used by permission and are the property of the original copyright owners.

Front cover photo: Cathedral Rock Reflection © Alexey Stiop/Dreamstime.com

Title page photo: biking near Sedona © Tom Grundy/123rf.com

Half title page photo: a fountain in Tlaquepaque Plaza © Kathleen Bryant

Printed in the United States

Moon Spotlight and the Moon logo are the property of Avalon Travel. All other marks and logos depicted are the property of the original owners. All rights reserved. No part of this book may be translated or reproduced in any form, except brief extracts by a reviewer for the purpose of a review, without written permission of the copyright owner.

All recommendations, including those for sights, activities, hotels, restaurants, and shops, are based on each author's individual judgment. We do not accept payment for inclusion in our travel guides, and our authors don't accept free goods or services in exchange for positive coverage.

Although every effort was made to ensure that the information was correct at the time of going to press, the author and publisher do not assume and hereby disclaim any liability to any party for any loss or damage caused by errors, omissions, or any potential travel disruption due to labor or financial difficulty, whether such errors or omissions result from negligence, accident, or any other cause.

ABOUT THE AUTHOR

Kathleen Bryant

© RICHARD MAYER

Kathleen Bryant was six months old when her parents bundled her up for her first road trip west, and she's been traveling ever since. At age four, after a winter in Tucson and Phoenix, she fell in love with the Sonoran Desert. Her memories include bouncing over dirt roads in search of ghost towns and having lots of picnics with green Kool-Aid.

Kathleen moved to Phoenix from the Midwest nearly 25 years ago, and she likes to say that she's still thawing out. She has also lived in Sedona and Tucson and has traveled extensively throughout Arizona in search of historic places, scenic vistas, good food, and interesting stories. Many of her favorite places to visit are in the red rocks and green woodlands near Sedona, but her love for the desert encompasses its cultures and cuisines as well as its landscapes. Starry skies, spicy food, rabbitbrush-lined roadways, and summer monsoon storms are some of the reasons why she calls the southwest home.

Kathleen has written a dozen books, including *Kokopelli's Gift*, an award-winning children's story. Her travel writing includes *Moon Grand Canyon*, *Moon Four Corners*, and the scenic guides *Sedona and Red Rock Country* and *Four Corners: Timeless Lands of the Southwest*. In *Western National Parks' Lodges Cookbook*, she combines her love of travel and history with recipes from landmark park lodges. She has also contributed stories to *American Archaeology*, *American Artist*, *Arizona Highways*, *Sunset*, and other magazines.